Antiques

IDEAL HOME MAGAZINE

TONY CURTIS

Charles Scribner's Sons
New York

Copyright © 1973 Lyle Publications

This book published simultaneously in the United States of America and in Canada – Copyright under the Berne Convention.

Printed in Great Britain
Library of Congress Catalog Card Number 74-3738
ISBN 0-684-13819-0

on a Budget

Contents

Colour Plates

Introduction

THE question most commonly asked about antiques is "How do you know that a piece is genuine?"

This is one of those questions which asks one thing and implies several others and, as such, is almost impossible to answer simply. The direct answer, of course, is that, according to most recognised authorities, an antique is an object made over 140 years ago but, with life and styles moving as fast as they do, almost every elderly object is nowadays tagged with the "Antique" label.

The implied questions relate to the style, quality and value of the article and, as regards these, there is no secret formula whose application will produce instant expertise. There are, however, a number of yardsticks against which individual pieces may be measured in order that their place in the scheme of things may be judged to within quite close limits.

The main purpose of this book is to offer some basic suggestions for the guidance of those who, while having an appreciation of the look and feel of antique furniture, lack either the confidence or the finance to plunge into collecting at the deep end.

The items I have chosen are, I think, representative of the middle section of the market and I have avoided wherever possible the kind of definitive description so beloved of antique "experts" which relate to those "classic" pieces which are rarely seen in any but the most exclusively expensive salerooms. Instead, I have tried to give some general pointers on the subjects of style and quality which may prove useful when they are applied to the kinds of pieces which are likely to be found in local shops and salerooms throughout the country.

As regards values of individual pieces, these vary considerably from place to place and are dependent to a great extent on the localised variations in fashionable taste. It is this local variation which accounts for the wide ranging activities of professional antique dealers and makes generalised pricing somewhat tricky. The prices given throughout this book, therefore, should be regarded as average saleroom prices, being calculated from recent auction lists gathered from all parts of the country and relating to pieces in average condition. It would be almost impossible to suggest shop prices, since these are determined not only by the cost of the article to the dealer but by the additional (and frequently considerable) cost of repair and restoration which must often be borne before the article is in a saleable condition.

For the totally inexperienced buyer, I would advise that a start be made by buying chairs from the late Victorian period which can, as experience breeds confidence, be sold at a modest profit and exchanged for something a little better. Do not waste your time and enthusiasm on the vain search for a set of Regency chairs for a tenner—the chances are that you will search for ever.

Do not be afraid to go into antique shops and look at the pieces offered for sale for, provided you treat their wares with respect, most dealers will offer no objection. But, a word of warning; do not pester dealers with endless strings of questions—their knowledge is their livelihood and, although they will usually be happy to give a few tips, they may understandably resent having their brains picked.

Beyond its purely aesthetic appeal, furniture of a bygone age frequently has one great advantage over that which is produced at the present time; it generally appreciates in value as each year passes and few people in this day and age would disagree with the proposition that beautiful furniture whose investment potential may be as high as that of property is an asset indeed.

Dining Chairs

POSSIBLY the greatest problem confronting a designer of chairs has always been that of creating a style robust enough to survive the dinner-time onslaughts of ebullient, 22-stone rugby forwards while retaining a degree of elegance which will endear his product to the most fastidiously feminine of maiden aunts.

Very few designers achieved this happy blend, most coming down on the side of strong practicality and a few (such as Sheraton and Hepplewhite) concentrating on a fashionable delicacy

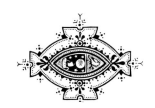

at the expense of strength. Chippendale was the man who came closest to combining the two elements and it is this which has made chairs based on his designs among the most popular

ever made.

Because chairs are the items of furniture to be found in the greatest numbers in most rooms, it is important that they should be chosen with care in order that they fulfil their utilitarian functions adequately without clashing with the larger pieces.

Fortunately, chairs have always been made in such numbers that every possible variation in style can be found and it should not prove too difficult to obtain those which will blend happily with your own particular decor.

EDWARDIAN PADDED BACK CHAIR

FOLLOWING the death of Queen Victoria in 1901 the country went into mourning and many furniture designers followed suit. This was the period renowned for its heavy, dull furniture, frequently stained or painted black (many householders, indeed, slapping a coat of black paint on every stick of furniture they owned, regardless of style or quality).

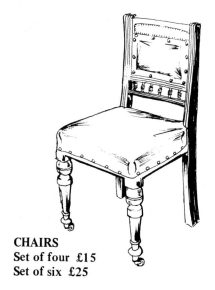

CHAIRS
Set of four £15
Set of six £25

This heavy chair is typical of its period, dull and drab with an over stuffed seat covered in leatherette pinned with oxidised studs.

Although these are rather uninspiring material, they offer a challenge to the ingenious homemaker who is forced to operate on a limited budget.

Unfortunately, they do not strip well, the dyes used during this period tending permanently to discolour the wood, and even the most determined bleaching usually results in a rather dismal grey colour. I am certain, however, that these obstacles will not prove insurmountable and that the means could be found to return the Edwardian style chairs to the dining rooms of the nation.

EDWARDIAN DINING CHAIR

ALTHOUGH reproductions of late 18th century designs were fashionable during the final quarter of the 19th century, Edwardian cabinetmakers, striving to simplify the creations of Sheraton and Hepplewhite for mass production methods, inadvertently

achieved a style peculiar to themselves. This style, now known simply as "Edwardian", generally calls to mind either massive, ill made, black monstrosities or beautifully inlaid pieces of incredible elegance, and in the main, this impression is correct—there was no middle way.

Singles £8
Set of four £65
Set of six £110

This little chair is one of the better pieces—not the absolute best but elegantly designed and nicely made in mahogany with satinwood banding and boxwood string inlay as fine, in my opinion, as any produced.

Although these may be covered in a variety of materials, I think plain fabrics are most suitable (moss or olive green being particularly effective shades) since these help emphasise the inlay work and do not compete with the design of the chair.

VICTORIAN UPHOLSTERED BACK CHAIR CIRCA 1870

THESE chairs became popular during the 1870s at which time the upholsterer's craft began to be more widely recognised than hitherto; most dining and armchairs of the period being padded and stuffed on almost every available surface (it was, perhaps, no coincidence that, as Queen Victoria matured and grew heavier, furniture design followed suit!)

The last of the truly Victorian chairs, this, later styles relying on the late 18th century for inspiration.

Set of four £27.50
Set of six £45

Anyone seeking an inexpensive set of comfortable antique chairs would do well to invest in these—they can be bought so cheaply at the moment that they are almost certain to increase in value.

Since chairs of this period were often made of good English oak, these (though somewhat heavy in appear-

ance) can adopt a totally new character if they are stripped of their dark polish and bleached almost white.

As regards upholstery, sombre colours are more in keeping with the original style though, stripped, they will cheerfully accept a surprisingly wide range of fabrics.

VICTORIAN BEDROOM CHAIR

THROUGHOUT the Victorian era, dining room chairs tended to be heavy and ponderously respectable in style, drawing room chairs being somewhat lighter and less stolid while bedroom or "fancy" chairs were sometimes positively frivolous.

This delightful little balloon back chair falls squarely into the bedroom category, being delicately feminine in style and obviously not robust enough to stand a great deal of masculine use.

Usually made of beech, sometimes left natural and polished but usually stained to simulate rosewood or mahogany, these chairs have cane or rush seats above slender turned legs with stretchers; you may occasionally come across an example having legs which turn slightly outward at the bottom.

Bedroom chairs may occasionally be found to be made of rosewood with delicate carving on the splat or, sometimes, they may be painted black with gilt scrolls and mother of pearl inlay on

Singles £6
Pairs £15

back, legs and seat. You could be very lucky to find one made of papier mache, though this should cost upward of four times as much as a wooden chair.

Nice chairs, these, but use them singly or in pairs; they are too fragile for the dining room, especially if you entertain members of the rugby club.

A typical selection of chairs in an Antiques Trade warehouse.

VICTORIAN GOTHIC CHAIR
CIRCA 1850

THE Gothic period dated from the latter part of the 12th century until the end of the 15th century during which time architectural styles (strong vertical lines, pointed arches and profuse ornamentation) were clearly reflected in furniture design.

Since that time there have been any number of Gothic revivals, notably by Chippendale in the 18th century and by A. W. N. Pugin who, in the following century, impressed his fellow designers with his furniture for the House of Commons and, in particular, with his display piece for the Mediaeval Court at the Great Exhibition of 1851.

Unlike Chippendale, who used the Gothic influence with restrained delicacy, the Victorian Gothic revivalists tended to build their furniture in a monumental style more suited to the cathedral than the home.

Set of four £35
Set of six £65

With the current trend towards smaller housing it is unlikely that Victorian Gothic furniture will ever return to fashion simply by virtue of its size and cumbersome style; put six of these in the average modern dining room and there would be no room to eat!

An odd chair can, however, be used to good effect as a space filler and will often add interest to an otherwise featureless hallway.

VICTORIAN ELIZABETHAN STYLE
CHAIR

ALTHOUGH balloon back chairs were the most popular in style throughout the Victorian period, a vast conglomeration of other designs also emerged; beside Grecian, Gothic, Sheraton, Hepplewhite and Windsor, with their assorted variations, a Victorian interpretation of the Elizabethan style was produced which vied with the balloon back for pride of place at the nation's dining table.

Majestically heavy, these chairs have high backs with barley twist columns and cane or (more probably) upholstered centre-pieces, over stuffed seats and turned or barley twist legs with stretchers. Consistent with the patriotism of the time they were made of good English oak and varied from being quite plain and inexpensive to having a welter of high relief carving (usually leaves and grapes).

Until quite recently these chairs were largely ignored (though many a November Guy has met his end enthroned on one) when foreign buyers, notably the Americans, realised that

Set of four £40
Set of six £70

they were exceptionally good value for money, since which time they have earned a great many dollars.

Slowly, however, people are beginning to realise that these are good, honest dining chairs and, covered in a tapestry or other suitable material, achieve a solidly pleasant effect set round an oak refectory table.

Designs for Ribband - back chairs from Chippendale's Drawing Book, circa 1760. The genuine Chippendale chair (right) closely follows his original ideas.

BENTWOOD CHAIR
CIRCA 1850

THESE elegantly practical little chairs were introduced into this country by the Austrian designer, Michael Thonet, at the Great Exhibition of 1851, who also introduced the Bentwood rocking chair illustrated right.

Usually having seats of cane or beadwork, bentwood chairs are simply constructed of beech which has been steamed and forced into a curve round an iron form (literally bent wood). Naturally enough, this method of manufacture was eminently suitable for mass production and vast quantities of these chairs were made, many of which have survived and can still be bought very cheaply today.

Beware of buying bentwood if the wood is split; the bending process puts a considerable strain on the wood, making repairs difficult, costly and seldom satisfactory. If the cane is damaged it can be repaired, though craftsmen who undertake this kind of work are becoming increasingly rare and it might be considered easier to

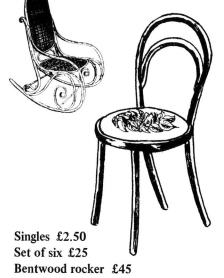

Singles £2.50
Set of six £25
Bentwood rocker £45

web the seat, apply a shaped piece of foam rubber and cover the whole thing with a suitable material.

I know traditionalists who will throw up their hands in horror, but I think these chairs are greatly improved if they are painted white and fitted with bright, attractive seat covers for, to be honest, they will never achieve high status as antique pieces of great merit and, in their original state, tend to be rather drab by today's standards.

VICTORIAN CABRIOLE LEG CHAIR
CIRCA 1850

THESE, I feel, are the nicest chairs to have been produced during the Victorian period, dating from about 1850 to the end of the century.

With their full balloon backs and French influenced cabriole legs these chairs achieved a degree of elegance soon to be lost as the popular taste turned towards more ponderous styles. The better made examples of this style were those produced at the beginning of their period of popularity and were usually of rosewood, walnut or mahogany, often with fine floral carving on the backs and knees and the most beautifully carved scroll feet; later chairs were often of beech or oak construction and not so well made or finely carved.

In my experience it is impossible to match these chairs, and my advice is not to waste time trying—I have never bought even two of identical design from different sources. This, of course,

accounts for the apparently disproportionate prices of sets, as opposed to single chairs.

Victorian cabriole leg chairs should be covered in velvet and, while deep buttoned seats are strictly correct for this style, dust does tend to collect in the dimples so it is often considered more practical to carry the material straight over.

If you should happen to find an odd chair with the centre splat missing, don't pass it by; if the back is filled in and deep buttoned it will make an ideal bedroom chair. Beware of attempting this with a rosewood chair, however, as this particular timber is hard and brittle with a tendency to chip.

Singles £10
Set of four £80
Set of six £225

SMOKER'S CHAIR
CIRCA 1840

THIS variety of chair rose to popularity right at the beginning of Queen Victoria's reign, holding its high place until the end of the 19th century. Usually made of elm, this chair has a saddle seat and turned legs which are splayed and braced with an H stretcher. The back is low and, with the arms, forms a crescent supported with from six to eight turned spindles.

Smoker's chairs can still be found virtually everywhere and they make ideal space fillers for, although there are so many of them, each achieves a

degree of originality from the attractively figured elm of seat and back.

Doubtless the name 'smoker's chair' derives from the fact that they were to be found in such numbers in clubs, pubs, barber shops and other predominantly male preserves, where Victorian gentlemen could gather and smoke away their Victorian problems without fear of spilling ash on, or burning, the upholstery.

Victorian smoker's chair £10

EARLY VICTORIAN BALLOON BACK CHAIR CIRCA 1830

MADE of either mahogany or rosewood, this chair provides the evolutionary link between the William IV style and the true balloon back of the mid Victorian era.

Set of four £50
Set of six £80

The turned legs have been retained, but they have become heavier and nearer the baluster style while the Grecian influence can still be seen in the carving at the top. The back, however, has undergone a radical change in that the yoke rail has become a continuation of the upright supports, which curve outward as they rise to meet it, and show signs of developing into the full, round curve of the true balloon back.

A good, sturdy chair, this, which can be covered to good effect in an extremely wide range of materials, leather, simulation leather, or good quality velvet being generally favoured.

VICTORIAN LATH BACK WINDSOR CHAIR CIRCA 1835

THE superabundance of Windsor style chairs of this period is due to the fact that almost every joinery shop in the country found them easy to produce from whatever wood happened to be available.

Singles £4
Set of four £22.50
Lath back armchair £15

The lath back style is by far the most comfortable of the Windsor chairs (the lath being modelled to fit the sitter's back) and the simplicity of the design enables it to blend fairly unobtrusively into any furnishing scheme while retaining an elegance which it is difficult to ignore.

The legs are always turned and braced with an H stretcher, two being frequently employed to give the added bracing necessary for an armchair.

Although these chairs were often stained to simulate rosewood or mahogany, they are much more attractive when stripped to show the true grain of the wood and wax polished.

The armchair variety can easily be fitted with rockers and, with an attractively covered foam rubber swab, will be surprisingly comfortable.

CHILD'S HIGH CHAIR

THERE are high chairs still in existence which date back as far as the 17th century but it was not until the 19th century that these really came into their own as universally established pieces of furniture. Widely varied in style, high chairs fall into one of two categories—"Town made" or "Country made"—and almost all were delightful and practical pieces of furniture, far more elegant than the clinically antiseptic plastic and chromium plated pipe constructions foisted on us by contemporary manufacturers.

The "country made" early 19th century hooped back Windsor chairs (usually made of elm) have holes in the front baluster legs to accommodate an adjustable foot rest, others being located in the arm supports for fixing a safety rail.

Windsor high chair £15
Victorian table-chair £40
Regency table-chair £75

The other "town made" examples follow the drawing room styles of their periods—notice the Regency style sabre legs on one and the balloon back and turned legs which place the third firmly in the Victorian period. The wood, too, generally tended to be consistent with that used for adult furniture of the period, mahogany and stained beech being most widely used.

Although the Windsor chair is made as a single unit, each of the other two is detachable from the table on which it stands and may be used as an entirely independent dining ensemble for the child.

VICTORIAN STEPLADDER CHAIR

THE boundless surge of inventiveness which marks the 19th century was not confined solely to massive engineering projects and mass productive factory machinery—there were a great many innovations of a more purely domestic nature and British homes began slowly to become gadget conscious.

Victorian stepladder chair £18

This Victorian stepladder chair is one of the more practical domestic products of its age which will still prove extremely useful in the modern household without having the drearily functional appearance of contemporary tubular kitchen steps. Usually made of oak (though sometimes mahogany) the design is usually fairly plain, though many show a Gothic influence and some are quite elaborately made with shaped back splats and fretwork sides.

Conversion from chair to steps is very simple; unhook the brass catches at the bottom of the chair, pull the back over towards the front and presto! four steps, high enough to change a light-bulb or reach a high shelf in perfect safety.

Always test the steps before you buy—remember that they might well be over 100 years old and may have sustained some damage in that time!

Victorian stepladder chairs are usually reasonably priced but, if you fancy something a little more elaborate and are well in with your bank manager look around for the Regency mahogany library chair variety. Illustrated here in the step position, they fold into an elegant chair and could set you back between £175 and £225.

WILLIAM IV DINING CHAIR CIRCA 1830

DEFINITELY a masculine chair, this one; heavy in design while retaining some of the elegance of the Regency period, soon to be lost in the cumbersome styles of the later Victorian era.

Early examples have turned and fluted legs which later become plainer as the fluting was omitted; the backs are waisted, nicely padded and set below the superb swirls and gadrooning of the yoke rail. Firmly established as a William IV style chair, this example still has a slight Grecian flavour of the Regency period while hinting at the future trend towards balloon backs and excessive weight.

Set of four £85
Set of six £200

Chairs of this period and style were almost all well made and of good quality mahogany or rosewood, sturdy and strong and easy to polish to a deep shine.

These chairs absolutely must be covered in leather (preferably real) and may be padded or studded. If, as sometimes happens, a set is found whose wood has a starved appearance, do as many professionals do and give them a good rub with dark tan shoe polish.

WINDSOR CHAIR CIRCA 1830

Singles £2.50
Set of four £15
Set of six £25

THIS down to earth kitchen chair, usually made of beech with a nicely figured elm seat, is one of the vast quantity produced from about 1830 until the end of the Victorian era. Widely used in the servants' quarters of larger households, the Windsor chair also proved extremely popular with the lower income groups and was to be found in the majority of working class homes, particularly in country districts.

While the legs retain the traditional, 18th century baluster turned style, splayed and braced with an H stretcher, the back uprights with their scroll over tops admit the influence of the Regency period. Better quality chairs were usually made with a rope twist splat in the middle or at the top of the back.

These are ideal with pine furniture and, if they happen to be painted (as often they are), they are still worth buying as it is quite a simple matter to pickle off the paint, sand them smooth and wax polish them.

Although they have saddle seats, I think they are often improved (particularly in terms of comfort) by the addition of one inch foam rubber seat swabs, attractively covered and fastened with ties to the back supports.

LATE REGENCY TURNED LEG CHAIR CIRCA 1825

THIS chair, while retaining a similar back to the Regency sabre leg chair, has adopted the more fashionable turned (or turned and reeded) legs of the period. Usually made of mahogany, better quality chairs are of rosewood and the sturdy design has ensured that they have survived to the present day virtually undamaged.

Set of four £100
Set of six £225

It is interesting to see furniture reflect the character of its age, this chair marking the move away from the elegance of the Regency period towards the formal respectability of William IV and Victoria. Suitable, therefore, for any household which aspires to elegance or feels itself to be on the brink of formal respectability, these chairs have either drop in or over stuffed seats which look equally good in striped material, velvet or leather.

REGENCY SABRE LEG CHAIR CIRCA 1815-25

USUALLY made of rosewood or mahogany, these chairs vary considerably in points of detail while conforming in overall style to the strong influence of classical Greece then in vogue. Essential features are the scroll over shape at the top of the back uprights and the sabre or scimitar shaped legs (curved, like the sword).

The legs may be reeded or plain; the seat may be drop in, over stuffed (the covering fabric being carried down and fastened beneath the seat, with no wood showing), or, occasionally, even of cane. The back should have either a bar support or a splat of rope twist design between the uprights and chairs of the really best quality will be inlaid with brass.

Chairs of this type and period are currently fashionable and command proportionately high prices but reproductions are made today and, although usually of beech, they maintain the same excellence of design and style while costing considerably less.

Naturally enough, the better quality chairs in this style were usually made of rosewood; but look carefully before you buy—some genuine period chairs were made of beech with a simulated rosewood grain. This can often be detected by an examination of the front legs and other places where rubbing is likely to occur, the distinctive figuring of rosewood giving way to the lighter uniformity of beech. Weight

should also be taken into account, true rosewood being one of the heaviest woods normally used in furniture manufacture, and considerably heavier and harder than beech.

Set of four £140
Set of six £300

WINDSOR WHEELBACK CHAIR

HAD there been a top twenty for chair popularity, the wheelback Windsor would undoubtedly have been consistently placed in the top three since the final quarter of the 18th century, for it was both simple to make and pleasing to the eye. In consequence it was made in vast quantities throughout the country, since it did not require the skills of a highly qualified cabinet maker.

The framework for the back was made from a length of wood, usually beech, which was steamed and bent to shape round an iron former before being fitted into holes drilled at the

An interesting Swiss, carved boxwood, occasional chair of oyster shape, circa 1840. £40

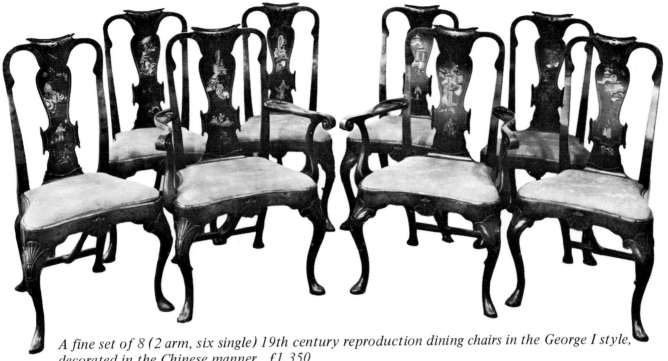

A fine set of 8 (2 arm, six single) 19th century reproduction dining chairs in the George I style, decorated in the Chinese manner. £1,350

rear of the saddle seat. The centre splat was traditionally fret cut in the shape of a wheel and on either side were three or four sticks from seat to hoop, two of which would be set at an angle for added strength.

**19th century Windsor wheelback
single £3
18th century Yew wood armchair £75**

They were usually of beech with nicely grained elm seats and were either left natural or stained black. If you go seeking these chairs, be on the lookout for early wheelback armchairs made of yew wood. Since the style has remained virtually unchanged, these can only be recognised by the attractively yellowish red of the wood which is often figured with a thin dark stripe and tight, dark whorls. A good Windsor wheelback armchair in yew can fetch anything from £50 to £100 while one made of beech can be bought for as little as £15.

SHERATON DINING CHAIR

THOUGH his designs have much in common with those of Hepplewhite, Thomas Sheraton (1751-1806), a drawing master from Stockton on Tees, much preferred straight lines to the curves favoured by Hepplewhite, his chairs achieving their feminine delicacy with their fine turning and slender frames.

Sheraton served his apprenticeship as a cabinet maker but he never actually manufactured furniture himself, concentrating on creating designs which he published in his *Cabinet Maker's and Upholsterer's Drawing Book (1791 - 1794)*.

While most surviving Sheraton chairs are made of mahogany, they can also be found in satinwood, painted white or gold or even japanned.

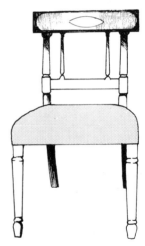

**18th century Sheraton chairs:
Set of four £185
Set of six £375**

The delicacy of this design demands that a fine fabric be used to cover the upholstery, green silk or satin being generally considered the most suitable.

More suited to the parlour than the dining room, these chairs must be treated with the utmost delicacy for, not being a manufacturer himself, Sheraton concerned himself more with the aesthetics of design than with the practicalities of use.

Although 18th century Sheraton and Hepplewhite chairs are expensive, Victorian reproductions will cost less than the price.

13

HEPPLEWHITE CHAIRS
CIRCA 1780

18th century Hepplewhite chairs:
Set of four £210
Set of six £425
18th century japanned armchair £130

THE Hepplewhite style is renowned for its flowing curves, shield, oval and heart-shaped backs and straight lines broken by carved or painted wheat ears and corn husks, all of which Hepplewhite adapted from the work of Robert Adam, the distinguished architect/designer and published in his famous guide: *The Cabinet Maker and Upholsterer.*

Another distinctive Hepplewhite design incorporated the three feathers crest of the Prince of Wales in the backs of chairs and he also favoured finishing chairs with japanned decoration of various ground painted with floral garlands, corn husks and medallions.

Yet another Hepplewhite characteristic is to be seen in the square, slimly tapering legs which were extensively copied towards the end of the following (19th) century and throughout the Edwardian era.

Beside the elegance of his designs, Hepplewhite is to be remembered for the explicit instructions given in his book regarding the materials to be used for the purpose of covering his chairs: for japanned chairs with cane seats, cushions covered in linen; for dining chairs, horse hair material which may be either plain or striped; for upholstered chairs, red or blue morocco leather tied with silk tassels.

CHIPPENDALE CHAIR
CIRCA 1750

THOMAS Chippendale designed and made furniture for the wealthy in his premises in St. Martin's Lane, London, establishing styles of his own rather than copying and adapting those of others. Like Sheraton and Hepplewhite, Chippendale published his designs, which were used by cabinet makers throughout the country, with the result that a considerable number of "Chippendale" chairs were produced in a variety of qualities and a medley of styles.

This example has flowing front legs (which, in the later "Chippendale" chairs, gave way to the easier constructed and more fashionable square legs with stretchers) and is nicely made in the rococo manner with plenty of fine carving and flowing curves. The centre splat is particularly fine and is surmounted with a cupid's bow top rail.

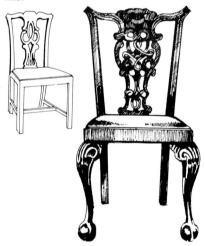

19th century reproduction Chippendale chairs: Set of four £85
Set of six £200

The prices I quote relate to Victorian reproduction chairs which have ball and claw feet and are made of beech stained to resemble mahogany. A genuine set of six period chairs could cost you well over £1,000.

Dining Tables

TABLES of one kind or another have been around almost as long as man himself. Originally little more than a plank on legs, the table gradually developed in shape and style to accommodate all tastes and permit a number of uses. Many, designed or found suitable for a particular purpose at a particular time, outlive the fashion which established their style, but most lend themselves quite happily to an alternative use to that for which they were originally intended. One of the more universal uses to which tables are put is that of providing a platform from which meals may be eaten and enjoyed. It is only common sense, therefore, to select for this purpose a table whose design and manufacture are of a standard that will enhance (rather than detract from) the fullest possible appreciation of a well cooked meal. The three chief factors to be considered when buying a dining table are size, appearance and stability and it is upon these three considerations that I have based the following selection.

CRICKET TABLE

MADE of either elm or oak, cricket tables were produced in great numbers throughout the 18th century and found great popularity among the working classes.

Besides being simple and sturdy in construction, the employment of only three legs in the design ensured that these tables would stand firmly on flagged or unevenly boarded floors as were often to be found in servants' quarters and poorer houses. The commonest examples will be found to have round, planked tops with tapered triangular legs splaying outward, while rarer varieties have turned legs and tops cut from a single piece of wood.

The name "cricket table" reflects its similarity to the small, three legged stools which, like our old friend Jiminy, were commonly to be found near the hearth or in inglenooks.

This makes an ideal occasional table, particularly when it is used as part of a simple, country cottage type of scheme.

ENVELOPE TABLE

FROM about 1750 until the end of the 18th century, furniture designers strove to break away from traditional styles in the attempt to create something completely different and this period saw a multitude of legs, flaps and movements built into tables which extended, opened, hinged, turned and folded up in order to achieve the maximum possible surface area in the smallest practicable space.

Cricket table with triangular legs £35

Cricket table with turned legs £45

Georgian envelope table £155

One of the simpler designs to emerge from this orgy of inventiveness was the envelope table—obviously so called from the triangular shape of the flap—which has all the attributes of a good Georgian table, being made of nicely grained mahogany and having cabriole legs and pad feet.

Made to stand out of the way in a corner of the room, the envelope table makes a useful card table or an adequate dinner table for two and has obvious advantages for those who dwell in small modern houses or flats.

DROP LEAF TABLE

THIS form of gate table has rectangular flaps which sometimes will be found to reach almost to the ground

Though essentially country made and of simple design, with straight, square legs chamfered on the inside edge, units of this kind were often used to form part of the large extending tables so popular throughout the 18th century—often with D-shaped tables fastened on to the ends.

Drop leaf table in oak £40
Drop leaf table in mahogany £60
George III sectional table
in mahogany £225

Made of both oak and mahogany the single tables can still be bought quite reasonably today (though not, I suspect, for much longer) and have the advantage of being able to seat

up to eight while folding away to no more than two feet deep.

Before buying, check the leg hinges for wear and wobble and examine the frame for signs of woodworm.

FOLDING TEA TABLE

ANOTHER product of the 18th century mania for extensibility, the concertina table is so called from the manner in which the frame folds in and out to accommodate the hinged top section.

Apart from retaining a degree of uniformity in the appearance of the piece, this method of extending a table enhanced its stability, since the flap rests not only upon two legs but also on the actual frame in the folded out position. The top, too, instead of dropping down the sides, folds upon itself in such a way as to disguise the fact that the table extends at all.

Folding tea table £125

Generally of mahogany, these tables are extremely neat and versatile. Use one as an occasional table, for cards, intimate dinners or, as the name suggests, for tea!

ELIZABETHAN ROOM

This reconstruction of a room of about 1600 is panelled in oak and furnished with sturdy un-upholstered chairs and finely carved chests.

Note the ground-level stretchers on chair and joint stool, the strong symmetry of the carving and the rudimentary turned decoration on the cradle and front legs of the chair.

The carved oak mantelpiece is from Albyns, Stapleford Abbots, Essex.

(Courtesy Geffrye Museum)

GATE TABLE CIRCA 1750

THE cabriole leg is so called from its likeness in shape to the leg of an animal (it's derived from the French word meaning "goat's leap") and implicit in the meaning is the suggestion of a free, dancing movement which would obviously be destroyed if stretchers were employed.

The change from gateleg to gate tables was a direct result of the switch in fashion towards cabriole legs and, once free of encumbering stretchers, the table's movement could be simplified in that two of the actual legs could now be swung out to support the flaps. This cleaned up the lines of the leg section by allowing the omission of the two extra "gatelegs" whose four additional verticals made the underside of the closed table look somehow impenetrable.

Gate table £150

The top of this table is either round or oval, the cabriole legs terminating in plain pad feet and the construction is of mahogany. Look for heavy tables of good quality wood with a rich, deep patina and as large a top as you can find.

Please remember that the patina has taken years to build up and can be destroyed in seconds by the thoughtless placing of a hot object on its unprotected surface. The only positive remedy for a ring left by a hot cup or coffee pot is to strip the polish back to the wood and start again, thus destroying the loving labour of many years and a correspondingly large part of the table's value at one stroke.

TRIPOD TABLE

Mahogany tripod table £40
Tripod table with birdcage £120

ALTHOUGH the use of three legs on tables was originally a purely functional element of design, it was inevitable that the fashionable designers should see the aesthetic possibilities of the style and exploit it to the full.

Although there were a number of country made, elm tripod tables manufactured, most of those available today date from the latter half of the 18th century and are of mahogany with a baluster turned central pillar into which are dovetailed the inclined cabriole legs with plain pad feet. Some, made from sophisticated designs by Chippendale, have delicate piecrust edging round the table top, magnificently carved pillars and fine bases with ball and claw feet.

These tables tip up, the hinged tops being secured by means of brass catches and, although they are fine for use as light tea tables, they are not substantial enough to be used for dining.

Look particularly for tops which revolve as well as tip by means of a "bird cage" at the top of the pillar and those with piecrust edging, elaborate centre columns and finely carved feet.

SUTHERLAND TABLE

THIS little table, named after Queen Victoria's Mistress of the Robes, Harriet the Duchess of Sutherland who died in 1868, is ideal for the smaller dining room for it will seat six when fully open yet, closed, will stand quite comfortably out of the way.

It has a narrow top and flaps reaching almost to the floor which, when raised, are supported on legs which swing out from the centre frame in a similar manner to those of the gateleg tables.

Made from about 1850 and continuing in popularity until the end of the 19th century, Sutherland tables were manufactured in a variety of woods; earlier examples are usually of rosewood and burr walnut, later ones employing walnut or mahogany.

Large walnut Sutherland table £75
Small inlaid Sutherland table £30

The smaller Sutherland table is an ideal coffee table and is made in the same variety of woods as the larger, dining, type. The later 19th century table, is beautifully made of mahogany, crossbanded with satinwood and inlaid with a conch shell in a central medallion.

An English, inlaid satinwood Pembroke table, circa 1780.

PEMBROKE TABLE

Pine Pembroke table (top left) £15
Pembroke table
with splay feet (top right) £475
Late 18th century mahogany
Pembroke table (centre) £80

attractive when stripped down to the pine, wax polished and established in the kitchen. But be warned if the wood has been stained rather than painted, the result is likely to be disappointing.

REGENCY SUPPER TABLE

THIS is basically a sofa table with the flaps being hinged from the long sides instead of the short, and having one long drawer in the apron with a dummy front at the opposite end

Usually made of mahogany or rosewood, the Regency supper table was popular from the beginning of the Regency period through to the start of the Victorian and, although there was little variation in the style of the tops, bases varied considerably in pursuit of changing fashions.

I feel strongly that these tables are underpriced at the moment, especially when compared to the prices fetched by sofa tables, for they are similarly elegant and equally useful; perfect for a candlelight dinner when three would be a crowd.

Look for the earlier examples with splayed legs and brass castors (later tables are less elegant and have either bun or paw feet), particularly those with wide crossbanding or, better still, brass string inlay.

THIS useful table, introduced during the 1760's, was, according to Sheraton, named after the Countess of Pembroke, who was the first to place an order for one.

Essentially, the Pembroke table has a rectangular top with a drawer and small flaps that are either squared or oval in shape. Beyond this, there are any number of different bases ranging from elegant centre columns with tripod splay feet to bulbous, turned pine legs as on the late Victorian examples.

Owing to wide variations in style and quality (price too!) Pembroke tables may be used anywhere from salon to toolshed.

The better examples make excellent dining tables for two, or four at a pinch, while, if you fancy a bit of stripping–paint, that is–the later Victorian Pembroke tables can be very

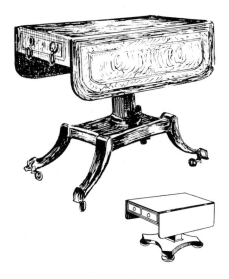

Regency supper table £140
Early Victoria supper table £60

SOFA TABLE

THE sofa table, was originally introduced to the world by Sheraton towards the end of the 18th century. He suggested that the length should be five feet six inches, (with flaps raised) the width two feet and the height 28 inches.

Basically, of course, this is simply the Pembroke table stretched a bit into more elegant proportions and it is interesting to consider how, given the fundamental idea of a table with drawers and flaps, three such successful designs as the Pembroke, sofa and Regency supper tables can be produced.

Earlier sofa tables were made of mahogany or, occasionally, satinwood but later, in the early 19th century a variety of woods was used including rosewood, amboyna and zebra wood. These are good tables in every sense of the word and, as such, command high prices. Although the 19th century examples are the more flamboyant with their use of exotic woods, inlaid brass and lyre end supports, it is the more austerely elegant late 18th century variety which are the most sought after and, therefore, the most expensive.

REGENCY BREAKFAST TABLE

I CANNOT fault this table in any way; it is beautifully designed, extremely practical and is always of superb quality.

Following the popular Regency style, the base comprises a centre column with four splayed legs terminating in brass castors. The top, pivoting by means of two thumb screws, may be quite plain or, as illustrated, have wide crossbanding and ebony string inlay and is shown to best advantage in the vertical position.

You get nothing for nothing and not much for sixpence. . . . .

Tables such as this seem frighteningly expensive but it must be remembered that they represent some of the finest work produced during one of the most elegant periods of our history and, if that is not enough, their design is eminently suited to the compactness of modern living space, ensuring that they will remain much in demand throughout the foreseeable future.

I might add that I have seen tables of this style with oval tops of figured elm and satinwood banding fetch prices as high as a staggering £1,000....

GATE LEG TABLE

THE gate leg table has remained one of the most popular styles ever since its introduction during the 17th century, even those being made today having the same basic design and movement as the originals.

Usually made of oak, though occasionally of more exotic woods such as yew or walnut, the majority of gate leg tables have tops of round or oval shape and the legs are braced with stretchers which, like the main frame, are cut to take the pivoting "gate" leg. (Larger tables are constructed with two gate legs on each side).

As a rule, prices reflect top size and, when the length of the closed table is greater than four feet, they really begin to soar into large figures.

Although these tables have been made since the 17th century, the vast majority date from the late 19th and early 20th centuries and these are virtually ignored by all except the shippers of antiques, who buy them in bulk and export them all over Europe and particularly to Holland.

A truly amazing transformation can be effected when a dull, drab late 19th century gateleg table is bleached, the edges of the top gadrooned and the whole thing waxed to make a really striking and very serviceable piece of furniture.

When buying, look for the older examples on which the dowels will be found to protrude slightly and check your diagnosis by examining the amount of wear on the underside of the top flaps—constant pivoting of the gate legs will cause considerable marking.

Regency brass inlaid sofa table (centre) £675
Rosewood sofa table (top left) £400
Sofa table with lyre ends (top right) £525

Regency breakfast table £300

19th century oak gate leg (centre) £20
17th century oak gate leg (top left) £255
Rare 17th century oak gate leg (top right) £1,400

Regency drum table £600
18th century drum table £800

Mahogany loo table £60
Rosewood loo table £90
Brass inlaid table £275

Marquetry loo table £425
Queen Anne marquetry card
table £600

DRUM TABLE

THE drum table, also known as the "library" or "rent" table, first made its appearance during the later half of the 18th century, becoming widely popular throughout the entire Regency period and remaining in favour until about the middle of the 19th century.

Earlier drum tables are of mahogany, Regency manufacturers also using rosewood. The Victorians continued to make them of both these woods but seemed to prefer burr walnut.

Often having revolving tops, drum tables were widely used in estate offices and the idea was that the agent could swivel the table top round in order to reach all eight or so drawers without moving from his seat (each drawer relating to a portion of the estate).

Although there are some eight to twelve drawer fronts round the circumference of the top, do not be surprised to find that a number of these are false—had they all been used to hold the rent money it is probable that craftier tenants would have paid their rent with one hand and dipped into someone else's with the other!

Due to its having been in constant use as an item of office furniture, you may find that an otherwise sound drum table is marred by a badly damaged top. Even though the wood itself is beyond repair, a transformation may be effected by having the top covered in tooled leather as many of the original pieces were.

LOO TABLE 1830

DESPITE unfortunate contemporary colloquial connotations of the name, loo tables make first class dining tables for up to six people.

Named for the three to five handed variant of whist which became a fashionable craze during the mid 19th century, the circular top and central pillar design of these tables made them the ideal surface on which to play loo; allowing the players to distribute

themselves evenly and comfortably without anyone being perched uncomfortably on a corner with lower limbs cramped against a table leg.

Usually made of mahogany or rosewood, they have turned or reeded central columns on a platform base with either bun, claw or lion's paw feet.

Since these tables are in plentiful supply and offer a great variety of detail, I suggest that it is worth spending a little time to find one veneered in rosewood or with a quarter veneered top as these are definitely the better investments.

Just occasionally you may come across one having brass inlay on the frieze and brass claw feet but these are likely to cost twice as much as their more common relatives.

One last tip; those having larger tops are usually better value than the smaller varieties.

MARQUETRY LOO TABLE 1840

DEFINITELY the creme de la creme of the loo tables!

Although the bases are generally the same as those on the plainer, burr walnut loo tables, the tops are usually either shaped or have scalloped borders and are most beautifully inlaid in various woods with birds, foliage and scroll designs similar to those of the Queen Anne period.

Incredibly beautiful as most of these tables are, I think that they are often overpriced and I would definitely advise that anyone operating on a limited budget stick to the burr walnut examples.

A few years ago, I heard tell of a dealer who spotted a marquetry loo table in a sale. It had been painted white all over but, just visible under the badly applied paint was a seductively beautiful marquetry flower.

He bought this table for fifty pounds and could hardly wait to get it stripped and repolished, knowing full well that the renovated table was going to fetch at least £200 and make him a nice little profit.

Imagine his feelings when it was discovered that the table had been in a fire at some stage and the top ruined apart from the small central area which had remained undamaged.

Hastily repainting the table (but making sure that the flower could still be seen through the badly applied paint) the dealer unloaded the table at a small profit on to another man with an eye for a bargain. . . . .

As far as I know, that same table is still doing the rounds, being regularly stripped, repainted and hastily sold; so, if you see a white table with a small, seductively beautiful marquetry flower just showing through the paint, you have been warned!

BURR WALNUT LOO TABLE CIRCA 1840

DURING the Victorian period, the style of these tables became more elaborate and the erstwhile plain centre columns and feet more decorative.

Tables of this period are nicely made with superbly carved bases and beautifully figured walnut tops which

Burr walnut loo table £115
Queen Anne burr walnut
card table £450

have a most useful tip up action operated by two screws placed underneath, making it possible for them to be stood out of the way when not in use.

Since the Queen Anne period, burr

walnut had been neglected but makes a successful reappearance on these tables, the best examples of which have boxwood string inlay and floral centre pieces.

These tables are generally of first class quality but, being made of walnut they are vulnerable to the ravages of woodworm. Do not necessarily let evidence of worm deter you from buying, however, since this can be treated relatively inexpensively provided it is not too widespread.

An interesting feature to be found on many tables of this type is the iron rod which, passing through the base, may be undone to allow the lower section to disintegrate into a multitude of pieces—useful when space must be saved in the removal van.

I once knew a Dutch dealer who specialised in loo tables (even his name was Lou), making regular buying trips to England. His proud boast was that, by thus dismantling his purchases, he could pack as many as 40 loo tables in his Ford Transit van—*Guinness Book of Records* please note.

The elegant dining room at Chandlers' Hall

22

WALNUT LOO TABLE 1860

AS the loo table developed, the top became more of an oval shape and the lower section was made rather more elaborate than hitherto.

The single, central pillar was enlarged into a cage of four columns and the rather plain splayed legs were often embellished with an amount of low relief carving. Although the tops were usually inlaid with box-wood, the quality of these tables fell off badly and, being made of walnut, they were very attractive to woodworm.

A number of tables were made in this style of ebonised wood with burr walnut decoration and, although these were generally of slightly better quality, they still fell far short of the standards set by the earlier loo tables.

Walnut loo table £40
Ebonised loo table £45

Truly, these are the worst of the loo tables and, unless an exceptional example can be found, I would recommend them to no one for, besides the fact that the polish is usually very bad, the construction of the bases was such that they are invariably unstable.

VICTORIAN CARVED OAK CENTRE TABLE

THE Gothic revival of the 1850s, following A. W. N. Pugin's exhibits at the Great Exhibition, brought about a resurgence of good taste for old English carved oak. It might be said that the motto of this period was "If you can't move it, carve it".

The feeling conveyed by furniture typical of this period is that of the solidity of the British Empire; patriotically made of English oak in a monumental style which seemed destined to last for ever.

Victorian carved oak centre table £90

Despite their weight—and I mean weight—these tables with either round or square tops, were usually so well made that they deserve more attention than those produced later in the period.

In line with the social behaviour of this era, the ponderously sombre appearance of the furniture often revealed, on closer inspection, a surprising amount of gay and irreverent detail.

If you like the shape of these tables but not the colour, I suggest that they be bleached and wax polished to reveal the richness of the natural timber.

REGENCY PILLAR DINING TABLE CIRCA 1810

THE design changed at about this time from the rectangular and D-ended styles to tables which were either round or sectional.

The latter were extremely practical tables for, besides allowing ample leg room, they could by the simple addition of more units be extended at will from four seaters to tables the length of a street.

Bases had plain or turned columns with three or four splayed legs which were either plain or reeded, terminating in brass castors

Since genuine pieces in this style are few and far between, those on a limited budget might do better to consider one of the many reproductions available which, of course, command only a fraction of the price of an original table.

Although repros are invariably made of beech and stained to resemble mahogany, they still maintain the excellence of line and many are very well made indeed.

Regency three pillar dining table £450
Regency four pillar dining table £800

VICTORIAN EXTENDING DINING TABLE

THIS is the table which, heavy and massive, most people instinctively associate with the Victorian period, despite the fact that the weight of the furniture during this period closely reflected the weight of Her Majesty (light at the start of her reign but increasing considerably with the passage of time).

This type of table, usually made of mahogany, though sometimes of oak, extended by means of a worm screw operated by a handle in the centre and allowed the addition of one or two extra leaves. Occasionally the centre leaf was equipped with drop-down legs as a means of providing extra stability when the table was fully extended.

Although these tables were usually well made, I cannot see them ever returning to fashion, purely on the grounds of size.

Edwardian refectory table £40

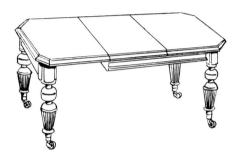

Victorian extending dining table £30

While these are unpopular dining tables, they are still widely sought by antique traders for the wood is of good quality and eminently suitable for use in the restoration of other pieces of furniture and the tops large enough for conversion into repro-duction Regency pillar dining tables.

REFECTORY TABLE

NAMED after the monastic dining rooms in which they were orig-inally used, refectory tables are based upon a very old design (students of history will remember that Henry VIII suppressed the monasteries during the years 1536–40, before which time they had enjoyed over one thousand years of establishment).

The name is now given to virtually any long table with legs on the outside edge although it originally applied only to those having six or more legs joined by stretchers at ground level.

Widely used until the end of the Jacobean period (1603–1688), refec-tory tables dwindled in popularity after that time, though they have been made in small numbers ever since right up to the present.

Elizabethan refectory table £425

While it is difficult and expensive, to pick up an early refectory table nowadays, there are a number of good reproductions of Elizabethan style available at quite reasonable prices and they are ideal for large families.

With long benches running on either side you have seating accommo-dation for a mini-banquet and, with food piled high and fresh fruit cascad-ing from wooden bowls, several bottles of wine and good company with whom to share it, these tables en-courage an evening of good mediaeval revelry.

Easy Chairs

A CHAIR, according to my dictionary is "a movable seat for one, with a back to it . ." and, by now, every man, woman and child in Britain must be aware that objects fitting this definition were used 3,372 years ago by the Pharaohs of Egypt at least (included in the treasures of Tutankhamun is a child's chair to make a collector's eyes gleam). Frequently of ivory or wood, expensively decorated and covered with animal skins, the early chairs were normally used as a symbol of high office, and were sometimes considered to confer special powers upon their owners or users. In mediaeval Britain chairs were used only by people of great importance who not uncommonly took them along when travelling and had them set up on a platform for use. Lesser mortals had to be content with stools, or cushions scattered on the floor. By the Gothic period, things had progressed somewhat and seats were often built into the structure of a room.

Indeed, some of the early chairs have the look of a section of the dining room wall! By the 17th century, chairs were really on the move and, by the end of the century, showed clear signs of wide European influence. In the following century, designs were imported from as far away as China and the roots were established for most of the styles which are to be found today. Where chairs are concerned, however, comfort is elsewhere than in the eyes of the beholder and this must, of course, be borne in mind when selecting a style for the home.

HORSESHOE BACK CHAIR, CIRCA 1880

THERE are any number of chairs with more or less horseshoe shaped backs but some have a rectangular padded section rising from the centre.

Horseshoe back chair £20

Although these are attributed to a design by one C. W. Trapnell, I think it is quite clear that the original influence reflects the Windsor smoker's chair of the 1840s, simply adapted to allow for the current taste for fat upholstery. While this is not the most immediately impressive of chairs, it can look quite charming with good upholstery and well polished mahogany or ebonised beech frame and makes a good standby to be called into service when your usual seating accommodation is fully occupied.

LATE VICTORIAN UPHOLSTERED ARMCHAIR

UGLY as sin and just as inviting, these are the chairs for anyone who is prepared to sacrifice everything for comfort's sake.

They are never to be found in antique shops because no self respecting antique dealer would even lift them up for the money they fetch but they can still be found in junk shops or, more probably, on the backs of passing dustcarts.

Despite this decided unpopularity, these are some of the most comfortable

**Late Victorian
upholstered armchair £15**

chairs to be found anywhere and are among the best buys of all time for those who favour a womblike environment.

Upholstered chairs of this type are plentiful, so it is well worth being a little choosy and selecting one with a good, sound frame and firm springing—It is never worth considering structural repairs since these will invariably cost more than the chair is worth.

Definitely at their best in a large room, these chairs lend themselves well to being draped in floral chintz loose covers with one or two well plumped feather cushions covered in a toning, self coloured cloth.

A word or warning—visitors who normally overstay their welcome will stay all night once you let them get settled in these chairs . . .

LATE VICTORIAN FIRESIDE CHAIR

ANOTHER contender in the ugliness stakes, this Victorian fireside chair has not even the quality of comfort to recommend it.

Generally made of mahogany, this chair is usually decorated with rows of bobbins somewhere; either under the arms or above and below the padded back and the turned legs invariably terminate in brass cup castors.

It is an interesting fact that chairs of this kind are sometimes bought by dealers just for the sake of the castors, since these are normally of a superior quality, ideal for many other, larger pieces of furniture.

Apart from this, the two main points in favour of these chairs are their strength and their cheap price (you may even be paid to take them away). The reason I include this chair is that I have a strong feeling that, in a few years' time, it is suddenly going to find itself back in fashion.

All that is really needed for this to happen is a Good Idea—there simply must be a way of making these chairs either comfortable or attractive—so far I have seen them painted white, stripped, bleached and with amputated arms but none of these, I fear, has had the desired effect but, if you are the kind of person who loves a challenge, good luck!

VICTORIAN NURSING CHAIR

THIS is one of a number of designs of small, more or less armless chairs which were intended for the bedroom.

Normally having beechwood frames with short, turned and fluted legs with brass cup castors, these are good, strong little chairs which normally radiate a peculiarly friendly feeling.

Designed for nursing mothers, the low seats and comfortable backs of these chairs are admirably suited to a relaxed position essential (so the books tell us) to the feeding of young babies and, in fact, the design has proved so successful that it has changed virtually not at all to the present day.

WICKERWORK CHAIR

WICKERWORK has, of course, been around as a country craft from the beginning of time but it was not until the late 19th century that larger items of furniture were produced in any quantity for the wider, urban market.

The word "wicker" comes from the early English word "wican" meaning "bend" and this, of course, accurately describes the method of manufacture; willow wands are bent and woven to produce a strong but fairly flexible object. Be it basket or chair the method is the same.

Largely neglected for some time, the majority of these chairs have long since been thrown on bonfires. Despite this, it is still possible to find one in quite reasonable, wormfree condition and all the treatment these need is a good scrub with soap and water and then, when completely dry, a couple of coats of polyurethane varnish. Non traditionalists might like to try one of

Late Victorian fireside chair £12

Victorian nursing chair £22.50

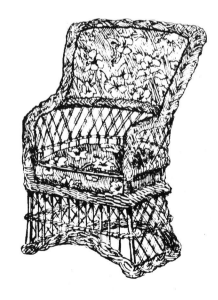

Wickerwork chair £10

the excellent, brightly coloured Hard-glaze range put out by Izal Ltd., under the Ronseal trademark.

Although wickerwork chairs tend to creak a little, they are very comfortable and, with a couple of bright cushions, very attractive and characterful.

VICTORIAN EASY CHAIR, CIRCA 1860

THIS is a good little upholstered chair with a well padded back, sprung seat and turned legs terminating in brass castors.

Upholstered chairs became extremely popular at this time and they remained so until the end of the 19th century. Their rise was partially due to the development of the helical spring which, for the first time, made it possible for the shape of the chair to be dictated by the upholstery rather than the wooden frame.

Victorian easy chair, circa 1860 £55

As a rule, the frames of these chairs will be found to be of ash or beech, the corners of the seats braced with wood blocks glued into place as a speedy and effective means of adding strength to a structure which, for almost the first time, was made to be totally concealed. The helical springs, mounted on the crosswebbed base in staggered rows, tied in such a way as to resist pressure applied from any angle, are covered first with hessian tacked to the frame all round, then horsehair and, finally, felt.

The backs of these chairs contain a lattice of iron bands (hence the trade term, "iron frame" chair) with one or two coiled springs in the centre and, occasionally, the chairs were made in the shape of an open oyster shell, the hinge of the shell forming the seat.

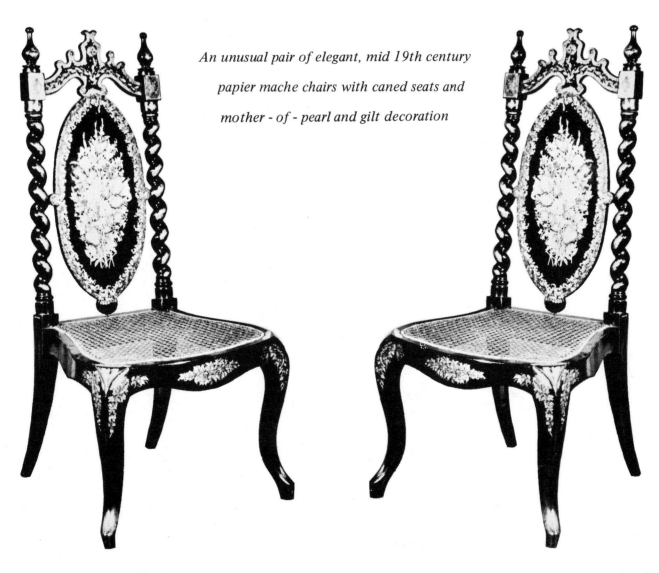

An unusual pair of elegant, mid 19th century papier mache chairs with caned seats and mother - of - pearl and gilt decoration

VICTORIAN TURNED LEG ARMCHAIR

THIS chair comes from the late Victorian period when styling seemed to give way to the economics of factory production—cost of manufacture, wastage of wood and full employment of machinery time evidently being considered of greater importance than elegance of line or even comfort.

Although basically the same shape as the earlier cabriole leg armchair, the rococo curves have here given way to a more rectangular line with turned legs and Gothic scratch carving - altogether easier and cheaper to manufacture.

Victorian turned leg armchair £50

Generally of poor quality walnut, the frames of these armchairs are very prone to worm, besides being weak at the points where the arms join the back uprights.

Although the better quality examples are fairly presentable chairs, they are decidedly second best to the earlier, cabriole leg chairs, even when nicely upholstered in good quality buttoned velvet.

ABBOTSFORD CHAIR CIRCA 1840

IN a style which has its roots in Cavalier England, the Abbotsford chair takes its name from the home of Sir Walter Scott whose historical novels were responsible for much of the feeling of romantic nostalgia which swept the country during the early to mid 19th century.

Made in a variety of woods, preferably walnut or rosewood, it has an overstuffed seat and short, stumpy legs with a high, Charles II type of back. The central panel may be either upholstered or of cane and the side rails plainly turned or barley twist with a

Abbotsford chair, circa 1840 £30

heavily carved cresting rail to add a touch of majesty to an otherwise somewhat disproportionate design.

Few would claim that an Abbotsford chair offered a high degree of comfort but, with a good beadwork or tapestry covering, a nice example will make an attractive filler for an awkward space in hall or dining room.

VICTORIAN OCCASIONAL CHAIR

THIS is another little armless chair whose high back, long low seat, short turned legs and brass castors are totally and wholeheartedly Victorian.

Cabinet makers of this period made the seats on some of their easy chairs very long indeed—no doubt to accommodate the copious bustles which were fashionable at the time and must have been somewhat difficult to manage on the seat of a more conventionally proportioned chair . . .

Occasional chairs like this were considered, rightly, as being ideal for displaying the art of beadwork which

Victorian occasional chair £50

was fashionable at that time and some are still to be found containing the most exquisitely realistic floral displays. In these days of instant everything, it is difficult to realise that some of these covers must have taken months and even years of painstaking and loving work in order to achieve a quality of workmanship which is unlikely ever to be seen again.

PRIE DIEU CHAIR, CIRCA 1840

ALTHOUGH this, like the Abbotsford chair, suggests a Carolean influence in its design, it is a Victorian adaptation and a classic example of the Victorian love of practicality, piety and well padded comfort.

Besides providing a very adequate seat on which to take Sunday tea (perched well forward, naturally, with fiercely crooked little finger) the prie dieu chair was designed to be knelt on, the T-shaped back having a flat top to accommodate the elbows. Seat, back and top were all well padded, to ensure that Victorian knees and elbows suf-

Prie dieu chair, circa 1840 £32.50

fered no discomfort in the service of their God, and were often covered in tapestry or Berlin woolwork; doubtless the result of many a Sunday afternoon's diligent embroidery on the part of female members of the family.

Some prie dieu chairs are found covered in remarkably fine tapestry or Berlin woolwork showing pictorial scenes of great beauty. If you should find one of these it is advisable to retain it in its original state but, if the covering is too badly worn, cover straight over with good quality velvet and either pipe or ruche the borders.

VICTORIAN OCCASIONAL CHAIR

THIS chair dates from the good period of Victorian furniture design, reflecting in the basic "S" shape of the frame the influence of Regency elegance. This has married quite nicely with the flow of cabriole legs and the overall line of the exposed frame has a pleasant fluency later to be lost beneath the fatter upholstery which came into vogue during the second half of the 19th century.

Victorian occasional chair £50

Made of rosewood or mahogany, these chairs are particularly striking when they are covered in a rich velvet (deep buttoned on the back and straight over the seat) but be very wary of covering one of the better quality rosewood chairs yourself since anything larger than a fine, half inch tack is almost certain to split the wood.

VICTORIAN ELIZABETHAN ARMCHAIR

THIS armchair is another product of the Elizabethan revival which occurred in the early years of the Victorian era and, bless them, the designers failed to get things quite right. Typically they incorporated most of the elements of Elizabethan design in the upper reaches of the piece and then slapped a pair of French cabriole legs on the front.

Features of this style are the high, padded back with barley twist columns on either side, a heavily carved cresting rail and shaped arms with a suggestion of padding on the tops.

Usually chairs of this style and period were made of English oak, though I have seen them made of mahogany, rosewood and walnut, all

Victorian Elizabethan chair £45

of which woods were widely used at this time.

These can be covered in virtually any material to suit the wood of the frame but, for safety's sake, I prefer to recommend a tapestry since this is definitely in keeping with the character of the piece.

Although the carved work is not usually very delicate, it is still inclined to damage fairly easily. Generally speaking, a certain amount of damage will not be noticed but, if you should wish to have a piece of carving replaced, always ask for an estimate first for this is inclined be a very costly work and "not too expensive" to a cabinet maker could well mean "astronomical" to anyone else!

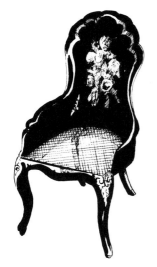

Victorian cabriole leg armchair £85

Papier mache chair, circa 1840 £110

VICTORIAN CABRIOLE LEG ARMCHAIR

THE mid Victorian period abounds with furniture showing the exaggerated curves and floral and leaf carving which clearly reflect the Louis XV rococo influence and this beautifully designed chair of the period simply cries out to be sat in.

Earlier examples had filled-in arms and rather plain frames of mahogany or rosewood but, within a few short years, they developed open arms and grandly flamboyant lines.

Walnut, being easier to carve, was widely used for the later chairs in this style and backs, arms, front rails and knees were adorned with welters of leaves, roses and bunches of grapes of superb quality.

Chairs in this style look best deep buttoned in a rich velvet and are particularly effective when the entire drawing room is full of matching furniture—quite often you will find suites in this style consisting of grandfather and grandmother chairs, a chaise longue and a set of six dining chairs. The complete nine piece suite looks really fantastic but be prepared to pay up to £600 to £800 and, if this seems a lot, remember that it would be money well spent, for complete suites like this increase in value at a faster rate than single chairs.

PAPIER MACHE CHAIR CIRCA 1840

ORIGINALLY a product of the East, papier mache made its European appearance in Paris. The process was patented (in 1722) by Henry Clay, of Birmingham, who used it to make mostly small objects such as tea caddies trays and jewellery boxes. It was not until the early 19th century that the firm of Jennens and Bettridge began fully to exploit the extraordinary lightness and flexibility of the material, producing papier mache canterburys, chairs, tables and even bed ends.

In the 1830s, Richard Brindley's manufacturing company helped to sustain the popularity of papier mache furniture until the middle of Victoria's reign, from which time it rapidly dwindled, lacking the strength and solidity which the later Victorians demanded of their household effects. Although papier mache can be made very hard indeed, it has little tensile strength, therefore wood is used for reinforcement.

The usual Victorian method of papier mache construction was to build up successive layers of paste-saturated paper over a mould and apply heat until a satisfactory degree of dry strength was obtained.

A second method was to pulp the paper and press it between heated dies. It was then shaped, varnished and hand polished before being decorated with mother of pearl and bronze powder or, occasionally, painted.

While papier mache furniture is difficult to repair, I have seen it done quite effectively with glassfibre (any of the many car body repair kits will prove quite suitable), painted with matt black paint and, finally, decorated and french polished.

VICTORIAN SPOON BACK CHAIR

THIS chair derives its name "spoon back" from the profile appearance of the waisted back which, being hollowed, may be thought to resemble a spoon, the effect being heightened by the way in which the back legs are set closer together than those at the front of the chair.

In better examples, the rounded top rail is embellished with a knot of rococo carving and the front cabriole legs are also carved, terminating in scroll feet with brass castors.

Beautifully proportioned, these chairs were extremely popular with Victorian ladies since the absence of arms ensured their suitability for displaying to best advantage the full dresses of the period.

In my view, this is among the best chairs to emerge from the Victorian period and, with its back covered in the original Berlin woolwork, or deep buttoned in velvet, it seems to make a place for itself in almost any surroundings.

Victorian spoon back chair £75

REGENCY "S" FRAME CHAIR

THE Regency "S" frame chair was made in a variety of sizes but, personally, I feel that the smaller examples have the greater charm.

Essentially a lady's or a child's chair, the design clearly reflects its introduction during the Regency period and the sweeping elegance of the flow from scroll over back through the seat to the line of the shaped legs ensure that chairs of this style maintained their popularity for about 50 years.

Being small, these chairs are primarily used as space fillers but young children seem to love them and usually claim them for themselves.

I have seen them made of rosewood but they are more often to be found ebonised with pressed brass roses on the four main points on the side. There are doubts as to their strength, since the design owes more to appearance than sturdy robustness. Despite this, a good example will withstand a considerable weight as was proved to me recently when visiting a dealer friend in his showrooms.

The largest lady I have ever seen in my life came in looking for a chair, complaining bitterly that there were so few truly comfortable chairs in which she could completely relax. Ignoring the large wing chair standing nearby, she made straight for this smallest of chairs and placed herself upon it, enveloping it completely beneath her galleon proportions, oblivious to my friend's strangled protest.

Struggling to her feet, she insisted that it was the most comfortable chair she had ever sat upon and, paying cash she sailed out of the showroom with her find clutched firmly in her hand.

WILLIAM IV ARMCHAIR

GENERALLY speaking, chairs have always tended towards the feminine at such times as they have departed from a line of strict neutrality in the battle of the sexes. Those made during the William IV period are the notable exceptions and this armchair was obviously made with no one but the man

of the house in mind.

Chairs of this period were occasionally made of rosewood but were usually made of mahogany of superb quality which polishes to a magnificent shine and colour. This particular example, of mahogany, reflects the Grecian elegance of the Regency period but it has a heavier and more established feel which will immediately appeal to the autocrat who still lurks within many a liberated male (what is this Women's Lib. thing, anyway?).

Bear in mind when buying such a chair that it is almost certain to dominate the room and that the man who sits in it is equally certain to dominate his household. Despite this, and its tendency towards heavy darkness, it does not have the aura of gloom and melancholy so characteristic of the weighty, late Victorian furniture.

Sit in it with dignity. Regardless of expense, cover it with genuine leather. Treat it at all times with the utmost respect, or I have the feeling that it might stalk out of your door in search of a place where it can uphold its Olympian position.

WING CHAIR CIRCA 1750

WING chairs have been made in this country since the 17th century, this being one of the few designs to have remained virtually unchanged since its conception, only the legs coming, going and changing shape according to the dictates of fashion.

The Queen Anne wing chairs had high cabriole legs canted from the corners which demanded extra stretchers for strength. The legs were later straightened and squared off with the inside edges chamfered, before the Georgian influence saw a return of the cabriole legs, but shorter this time and terminating in ball and claw feet. Most modern reproductions follow the Georgian style but my personal preference is for the square legged version illustrated right, and dating from about 1750

This chair's shape is determined by the frame beneath, for there is very

Regency "S" frame chair £45

William IV armchair £80

Wing chair, circa 1750 £220

31

little padding apart from the comfortable back and seat.

Ideal for draughty rooms, wing chairs convey a great sense of secure well being to all who sit in them and lend themselves easily to being covered in almost any material.

COCKFIGHTING CHAIR

ALTHOUGH this is an expensive chair and unlikely to be used for its original purpose, I feel that it is worth including here for its rarity and interest value.

Made of mahogany, this chair has a leather covered padded seat which narrows considerably towards the back, allowing the 18th century sportsman to sit astride, facing the back, with his tail coat hanging elegantly and uncreased. The elbows were placed on the suitably flattened and shaped crest rail and the adjustable easel was conveniently situated to allow scoring.

Cockfighting chair £375

Talking about cockfighting, there is an interesting fact, not generally known, concerning the treatment of any who welched on their bets.

Above the arena was suspended a wicker basket on a pulley and any enthusiast who failed to pay up promtly was placed in this and hoisted to the ceiling where he would remain until such time as he could make adequate assurances to his creditors.

32

BERGERE CHAIR
CIRCA 1760

THIS is a good, genuine Louis XV chair which, because the arms are a continuation of the back, hugs the body and proves very comfortable to sit in.

The frivolity of the rococo style was taken to extremes by the French cabinet makers but, in this chair at least, comfort was not sacrificed to style, though it is a beautifully elegant piece having fine French cabriole legs both back and front, and a nicely shaped front rail.

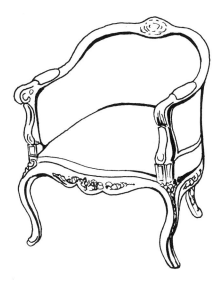

Bergere chair, circa 1760 £270

Like the last example, this genuine chair commands a high price but it was reproduced extensively during the Victorian period (particularly in the latter half of the century) and these can be bought for about £75.

So successful was this style that it is still used by manufacturers, though present day versions of the chair are usually made with cane backs and loose cushions.

CHIPPENDALE ARMCHAIR
CIRCA 1755

THIS armchair by Thomas Chippendale is, I believe, one of the best chairs ever made. Beautifully constructed to a superbly elegant design, it is strong, graceful and comfortable; a truly classic example of everything a chair should be.

The strong rectangle of the back is softened by the flow of the humped top rail and the arm supports, moulded and richly carved with feathers, terminate in cabochon ornament above the graceful acanthus carved cabriole legs with claw and ball feet.

**Chippendale armchair,
circa 1755   £400**

Although this is a genuine chair of the period, there were a number of copies made throughout the 19th century and, while these tend to be plainer with less rococo ornamentation, they still maintain the same style.

Do not waste time trying to find a genuine chair of this type—the only time most people see one is when they are visiting a stately home.

I remember visiting such a place in Sussex and rapturising over one of these chairs displayed in the Baronial Hall—only to be completely bowled over when, entering the Long Hall, I was confronted with about 23 matching chairs, all in perfect condition and each one worth a fortune.

But the Dook wouldn't part wiv'em!!

*A most unusual, walnut - framed chair bearing a patriotic portrait
of Prince Albert in the medallion back.*

Writing Desks

THE writing desk was born in the monasteries of the Middle Ages, originally as a small, Gothic style oak box with a sloping lid hinged at the back like old fashioned school desk tops.

As time passed and men of letters increased their output, the writing box grew and was made a permanent fixture in the copying rooms of the monasteries, being built upon a stand, usually high enough to be used by a man standing or seated on a high stool.

Later, the hinges of the lid were moved from the back to the front, allowing the lid to fall forward on supports and form a writing platform in the open position.

The practice on the Continent was to cover this area with a "burel" or russet cloth, probably named from the latin *burrus* (red), the colour of the dye used in its manufacture. It is doubtless from here that we gain the word bureau, though the connotations of the word have changed somewhat since it was first coined.

The bureau remained little more than a box on a stand until the close of the 17th century when it was married to a chest of drawers for obvious practical reasons. From that time onward, there have been few changes in the design beyond relatively small stylistic alterations which were reflections of the changing tastes of the fashionable rather than modifications dictated by practical usage.

REGENCY PERIOD DAVENPORT

THIS is a very delightful little desk which originated during the final years of the 18th century.

Primarily a lady's desk, it is one of those rare pieces in which the virtues of practicality and elegance are beautifully combined to produce a comfortable yet compact piece of functional furniture,

and a piece most conducive to the elegant penning of gracious invitations and romantic sonnets.

Earlier davenports such as this were usually made of rosewood or satinwood and were boxlike in structure apart from the sloping top which would either pull forward or swivel to the side in order to make room for the writer's lower limbs. They stand on bun, small turned or, occasionally, bracket feet and better examples sport a fine brass gallery to stop pens and small objects from falling down the back.

Davenports are now commanding high prices being ideal for the small houses and sardine can flats in which we seem increasingly to live.

While most examples are about two feet wide, it is well worth looking for the smaller ones (about 15 inches to 18 inches wide), for these can fetch twice as much as the larger models even though they usually have only a cupboard at the side instead of drawers.

WILLIAM IV DAVENPORT

IT was during the William IV period that the davenport gained its name and its popularity.

The story goes that one Captain Davenport placed an order for one of these writing desks with Gillows of Lancaster, a well-known firm of cabinet

Regency period davenport £225

William IV davenport £135

makers at the time. Known during its manufacture as "the Davenport order", the first desk was completed and the name stuck, being applied to all subsequent orders for a desk of this particular style.

The sliding top of the earlier model has given way to a fixed top which protrudes from the main body of the piece. This, in turn, stands upon a plinth fitted with either bun feet or castors. One side is fitted with four or five drawers and these are matched by a similar number of dummy fronts on the opposite side. Above these can often be found pull-out slides for extending the writing area. The protruding top is supported by either carved brackets or pilasters which, on the better examples, have brass capitals. When the writing flap is raised it will reveal a well, pigeon holes and small drawers which are usually veneered in satinwood as a contrast to the mahogany or rosewood normally used for the outside surfaces.

Pay particular attention to any space which cannot easily be accounted for; the designers of this period had a mania for secret drawers which can be revealed by catches concealed behind the conventional drawers or by sliding aside the panels separating the pigeon holes.

Do not expect to find any treasure, however; you are unlikely to be the first to discover the secret drawer. If you are in luck, you might find a curl of hair tied with ribbon, romantic evidence of a past love.

VICTORIAN DAVENPORT CIRCA 1850

DAVENPORTS were, at the middle of the 19th century, at the height of their popularity and at peak quality for, although they remained in vogue to a certain extent for the remainder of the century, the standard of workmanship employed in their construction declined steadily, never again to reach the level displayed in this and the other two examples illustrated.

Models after the style of the one illustrated were nearly always veneered with burr walnut (cut from malformations in the trunk of the tree) with its fascinating swirls and configurations, later pieces usually being of plain walnut which, although finely grained, lacks the flair of the burr variety.

Beneath the flap at the top of the desk was provided a compartment for paper and envelopes. Provision being made, too, for a pair of glass inkwells which normally contained red and black ink for use on the household account books. There is usually a hinged pen drawer at the side, capable of being turned to any reasonable angle for the convenience of the writer and the desk stands on finely carved cabriole leg supports.

Victorian davenport, circa 1850 £160

Although the davenport's basic style remained unchanged there were, of course, variations in points of detail; the front edge of the top could be straight or serpentine shaped and a better example had a top similar to that of a piano in shape with a rising compartment at the back which was operated by a catch concealed behind one of the small drawers in the well. This type, known as the 'piano top' davenport, also had a tooled leather covered pull-out slide for a writing surface.

EDWARDIAN OAK BUREAU

SMALL bureaux of this type have been made consistently from the turn of the century until the present day and they still, unfortunately, show no signs of fading from the scene.

The Edwardian oak bureau embodies a conglomeration of styles derived chiefly from the William and Mary period, with its barley twist legs, and the Stuart period with its applied moulding on the flap.

Generally poorly made, bureaux of this type have little to recommend them aesthetically, but they are functional and adequately serve the purpose for which they are made, though, if the Regency davenport is conducive to the penning of elegant phrases, I fear that these bureaux are likely to inspire little more than notes asking the milkman to deliver only one pint tomorrow please.

Edwardian oak bureau £15

Although I find words of praise for this style of bureau difficult to utter, I must confess that, faced with an unavoidable choice, I would always prefer to share my home with one of these rather than one of the characterless, pseudo-wood abominations foisted upon us under the euphemistic label of Contempory Furniture.

In fact, an Edwardian bureau, chosen with care, stripped, bleached and waxed can, in the right surroundings, look not unattractive, and will serve a useful purpose.

EDWARDIAN INLAID MAHOGANY BUREAU

ALTHOUGH this type of bureau is classed as Edwardian by members of the antique trade, it actually started its life during the revival, towards the end of Queen Victoria's reign, of the 18th century styles and fashions.

Veneered in a mellow brown mahogany, the drawers and flap are decorated with boxwood string inlay. Normally having three long, graduated drawers, better examples occasionally have four, both kinds being furnished with brass loop handles.

The writing flap, supported on slides positioned on either side of the top drawer, opens to reveal what is to me a rather disappointing interior, being a simple construction of plain oak as opposed to the finely craftsman-made interiors more commonly found in the earlier, 18th century models.

STUART ROOM

This room in the style of Sir Christopher Wren, comes from the Master's Parlour in the Pewterers' Hall and contains furniture of the Stuart period (c. 1668).

Undoubtedly sturdy though it is, the furniture shows some evidence of having been designed rather than just made: notice the angled front legs of the settle carrying through to the supports for the shaped arms and the hide covered chair in the foreground with padded back and seat.

There is an interesting child's high chair by the fireplace.

(Courtesy Geffrye Museum)

Edwardian inlaid mahogany bureau £75

The normal width of these is 2ft. 6in. to 3ft. but a few were made to a width of only 2ft. and these smaller ones are really attractive, though they will normally cost up to 75 per cent more than the larger pieces.

Look, too, for bureaux with elaborate inlay work on the drawers and flap depicting garlands of flowers, urns and corn husks. Being particularly fine, these are likely to cost twice as much as the standard models but they are sure to appreciate in value at a very satisfying rate.

GEORGE III MAHOGANY BUREAU

THIS must surely be the most attractive of the bureaux to be found in any numbers today.

George III mahogany bureau £185

Made of mahogany from about 1760 to the first quarter of the 19th century, it shows excellent proportions and is beautifully constructed on an oak carcass. The drawers, too, are oak lined and the interiors generally are particularly fine with an abundance of pigeon holes and small drawers decorated with boxwood string inlay and bone or ivory handles.

The flap was always made from a piece of mahogany, specially selected for the beauty of its figuring and finished with a lip moulded edge and brass escutcheon. Stamped brass handles, splayed feet and a shaped apron combine to ensure the overall attractiveness of the piece which is sometimes enhanced further by the inclusion of a centre cupboard in the interior, inlaid with a conch shell design and flanked by "secret" drawers made to resemble book spines.

As with many other pieces of furniture, size plays an important role in determining the market value of these bureaux, the larger, four foot wide models fetching less than their smaller rivals.

Once the width falls below three feet, the price can be expected to escalate rapidly with every half inch by which the size is reduced; remember that "the smaller the better" and you will be on the right lines.

SECRETAIRE CHEST

A SECRETAIRE chest is, basically, a chest of drawers whose deep fitted top drawer has a fall front which pulls forward to allow a sizable writing area with room below for the knees.

Having been made from the last quarter of the 18th century until the present day, they are to be found in an extremely wide range of styles, qualities and prices but Victorian varieties, having straight fronts and cupboards below the secretaire, can be bought for as little as £45.

My own preference is for the example illustrated over—a really beautifully proportioned piece of furniture and all that a secretaire should be. Made in the late 18th century, it is built of mahogany and has a serpentine front, shaped apron and slightly splayed feet.

Secretaire chest £400

When buying such a chest it is wise to bear in mind the similarity between it and a chest of drawers—you might well be buying an old chest of drawers which has undergone a modern conversion job!

Look carefully at the sides of the secretaire and the depth of the top drawer; the sides need to be thicker and stronger for a secretaire than an ordinary drawer, therefore a conversion will show if the sides appear to be of newer wood than those of the other drawers. The depth of the top drawer should be the largest in the chest and

marks will show on the side of the carcass where the supports have been altered to achieve this.

I would be just a bit suspicious, too, if the brass fittings appeared just that bit bright and shiny—they should look as though they have been around for a good few years.

SECRETAIRE WELLINGTON CHEST

THIS is a particularly useful piece of furniture, named after the Iron Duke and made from about 1815 until the middle of the 19th century.

It is generally made of mahogany but better examples are veneered in rosewood (which comes from Brazil or India and takes its name from the beautiful fragrance exuded by the freshly cut wood).

A tall, narrow chest, this has six to eight drawers which may be locked by a device on the side. The second and third drawer fronts down are occasionally false and made as one unit which drops to form a writing platform, revealing numerous small drawers and pigeon holes behind.

This truly elegant chest looks

its best when veneered in rosewood, the rich veneer polished to a deep shine to reveal the full beauty of the dark, reddish brown figuring.

Wellington chest £110

In these days of relatively confined living, the extra drawer space provided by pieces of this kind is always useful, particularly to collectors of small items; for these may be displayed to advantage in the many drawers and also kept safe under lock and key between times.

This is the magnificent writing desk at Nostel Priory.

38

REGENCY SECRETAIRE MILITARY CHEST

MILITARY chests were regulation issue for all officers in the Army and Navy from about 1815 to 1870 and, while retaining a common basic shape, they vary in quality and detail.

Being essentially practical rather than decorative pieces of furniture, military chests were made in the form of rather plain chests of drawers which could be divided into halves at the blast of a bugle and slung on the back of a nearby mule or coolie for transport to destinations new. Hoisting and carrying was facilitated by brass or iron handles set into the sides of each half.

Regency secretaire military chest £200

Regency examples may be found made of mahogany, teak or camphorwood with brass straps and corners and sunken brass handles on the drawers, the latter being occasionally discreetly decorated with ebony or brass string inlay. Better examples have a secretaire in one of the drawers in the upper section which drops down by means of catches on the sides to reveal a multitude of small drawers and pigeon holes.

Later Victorian military chests were nearly always of mahogany, had fewer brass fitments than the Regency variety and often had sunken wooden knobs instead of brass handles. These will cost about a third of the price of the camphorwood models.

There was a whole range of furniture manufactured in the military style, even to the extent of superbly made camphorwood and brass collapsible toilets complete with brass carrying handles. Recently, at the Bermondsey Antique Market, I saw one of these for sale which had undergone a discreet conversion: it now dispenses a glass of beer each time the flush handle is operated . . .

QUEEN ANNE ESCRITOIRE

THE name escritoire (or, scritoire as it was originally) was applied to the piece of furniture produced towards the end of the 17th century in answer to the demand for a cabinet with a falling front; prior to this time, all larger pieces had been equipped with double doors.

Although this design has been used ever since with only minor variations, it has never achieved the overwhelming popularity attained by some of the other writing cabinets and desks. The upper level, revealed by dropping the front, contains a multitude of drawers with pigeon holes above. The drop front, in the lowered position, is supported by a pair of brass jointed stays and has, mounted on its surface, a leather covered, adjustable writing slope.

The lower section contains three long, graduated drawers with brass drop handles and the piece stands on plain bracket feet.

Queen Anne escritoire £700

If you should find one of these, pay particular attention to the swell frieze as this will often be found to conceal a secret drawer.

The example illustrated above is made of burr walnut and is fairly standard in its details; some escritoires of this period may be found on a six-legged stand with shaped stretchers and a row of extra drawers in the frieze.

A delicate, eighteenth century walnut writing desk with elaborate marquetry decoration.

19th CENTURY MARQUETRY ESCRITOIRE

THIS fine marquetry escritoire, most probably of Dutch manufacture, has evolved slightly away from the older style which resembles a converted chest of drawers and is developing the more widely accepted escritoire design, the drawers being somewhat shorter and set about three inches in from the sides of the frame.

Marquetry was found in Italy in the 16th century and had spread across Europe by the last quarter of the 17th. It is made by sandwiching different veneers of wood (some being specially dyed for the purpose) and cutting carefully through all the layers, following a design drawn on the top surface. Taken apart, the veneers are then glued on to the carcass of the furniture, which is most probably of pine, the capes of one colour being exactly fitted to the bays of the next. There are a great many marquetry designs, but the most widely found are of floral displays which are often further embellished by the addition of such materials as mother of pearl or tortoiseshell.

Pay great attention to the siting of this piece of furniture in a room as it is particularly vulnerable to extremes of temperature or humidity. Bad conditions tend to cause pieces of veneer to lift and these are soon pulled off by children or contact with garments. When this happens, the loose pieces are invariably stowed carefully in a safe place in the fond belief that they will later be glued back—they never are.

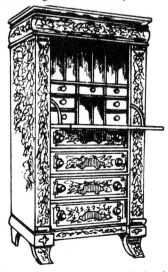

19th century marquetry escritoire £275

A fine Victorian piano - top davenport veneered in highly figured burr walnut.

VICTORIAN
MAHOGANY ESCRITOIRE

THIS somewhat ponderous Victorian escritoire, made about 1850, was virtually ignored until the Victorian boom of a few years ago.

Standing on vase-shaped feet, this piece is fitted with slightly protruding drawers having finger grooves on the underside to allow opening without the use of the heavy wooden knobs which would otherwise have been employed. In addition to the lower and interior drawers, there is a long drawer above the drop front and another, concealed "burglar" drawer in the frieze above.

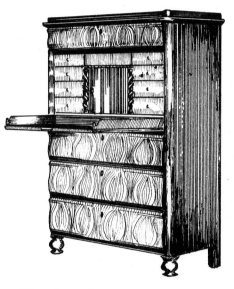

Victorian mahogany escritoire £90

It is a sad fact that some elderly people are forced to sell their treasured possessions from time to time in order to keep abreast of the rising cost of living. A dealer of my aquaintance used to buy regularly from an old lady who would never admit hardship but used to call him each year within a few days of the rates bills being delivered.

One year, he bought a piece from her, similar to the escritoire above. During the course of renovation, he became intrigued by the lack of depth of the interior drawers which suggested that there might be a hidden compartment between these and the back of the escritoire. Sure enough, a panel behind the drawers was removable and revealed a duplicate set of drawers containing old letters and documents—

and a leather purse containing a number of sovereigns.

Contacting the old lady, he returned these to her (really!) and she sold them to a specialist dealer for just over £600, insisting that my friend accept half the money.

She still makes her yearly sale and the dealer continues to buy from her, but at specially high prices nowadays.

TAMBOUR TOP DESK,
CIRCA 1800

BETWEEN 1775 and 1825 there were a number of beautifully made desks designed in a delicately feminine manner yet strongly built so that many have survived in good condition to the present day.

There is a fascination in any piece of furniture which has an action like that which is incorporated in this desk, for, when the drawer is opened, the tambour automatically rolls back into the frame to reveal a fitted compartment which may be used for storing paper and envelopes. The drawer also acts as a support for the flap, which can now be lifted from the centre of the desk and folded forward to provide an ample, leather covered writing surface.

Tambours were widely used during this period, both vertically and horizontally, to cover everything from desk tops to night commodes.

Made of thin strips of wood glued on to a linen or canvas backing, they run in grooves on the frame and follow any path the cabinet maker wishes them to take.

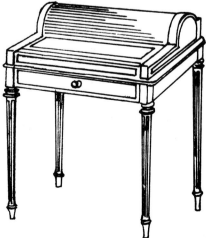

Tambour top desk, circa 1800 £285

Fortunately, tambours are quite easy to make, so do not disregard a piece of furniture with this section missing or damaged; simply buy a few lengths of ⅜in. half round ramin from your local do-it-yourself shop, cut them to size and glue the pieces on to a light canvas backing.

When the glue has dried, sand, stain and polish your new tambour and feed it into the groove from the back.

19th CENTURY
LADY'S WRITING DESK

THIS is a good quality 19th century lady's writing desk made in the late Louis XV style.

19th century lady's writing desk £170

Veneered in rosewood, it has a polished mahogany interior and the small, shaped flap is decorated with fine marquetry flowers and is cross-banded (the band of veneer on the border is set with its grain at a constant angle to the edge).

The square cut French cabriole legs have fine ormolu mounts on the knees and these extend, with a brass strip on the outside edge of the leg, to the ormolu toes. A fine, pierced brass gallery completes the top.

These desks are also found with plain flaps and these should be about £25 cheaper than their more decorated sisters.

If any of the ormolu mounts are missing do not despair, for new ones can usually be found after a bit of a search. These will be of polished brass but they look fine when they tone down with time.

VICTORIAN BAMBOO WRITING DESK

HERE is another piece of furniture peculiarly Victorian and not to be confused with the simulated bamboo wood turning popular during the Regency period.

A multitude of articles (canterburies, screens, hall stands and desks) were made of bamboo during this period, often combined with wickerwork and cane and, since the goods were not themselves much imported, many local craftsmen throughout the realm were busy producing tailor-made bamboo furniture to individual designs. The reason for this phenomenon was the craze for the Japanese look which swept the country, influencing designs of just about everything from china to fabrics.

While bamboo pieces are inexpensive and, therefore, buyable, I feel they tend to look rather out of place when mingled with the more conventionally made furniture. If you have, however, the desire to create a room full of eastern promise, there are enough pieces of bamboo furniture surviving to manage this quite effectively when blended with oriental style fabrics, wall hangings and laterns. To each his own . . .

Victorian bamboo writing desk £28

CARLTON HOUSE TABLE

THIS is an elegant and highly desirable writing table which was made from the end of the 18th century until about 1825 and then again during the Edwardian period when the styles of this era were revived.

Described by Sheraton in his Drawing Book as "a Lady's Drawing and Writing Table" it adopted the name Carlton House table from the residence of the Prince of Wales for whom the design was originally prepared.

Basically a D shaped table on fine square tapering legs terminating in brass cup castors, this particular writing table has a bank of drawers and compartments ranged round the sides and curved back and is usually made of mahogany or satinwood.

Carlton House table £750

Just occasionally, the centre portion of the Carlton House table slides forward or is adjustable to permit a more comfortable writing angle.

While the original period pieces are on the expensive side, good Edwardian copies can be bought for about a third of the price but even these are hard to find.

Although the fineness of the design makes this appear a small and elegant piece of furniture it is, in fact, quite wide and should be placed in a fairly large room if it is to be allowed to achieve its full effect.

VICTORIAN BURR WALNUT WRITING DESK

THIS is another fine piece of furniture; hard to come by but not, in my opinion, overpriced as yet.

Victorian burr walnut writing desk £425

It is veneered in burr walnut and is nicely shaped after the French style with ormolu mounted cabriole legs and a pleasant super-structure of drawers on either side of a central domed cupboard.

Apart from the styling, the cabinet making itself is really to be admired and I never cease to be amazed by the rapid decline of craftsmanship which occurred in the years following the production of this kind of furniture.

An ormolu mounted piece like this requires great care in the cleaning. The word ormolu derives from the French *or moulo*, ground gold, and the original ormolu as used by the 18th century French cabinet makers was, indeed, ground gold mixed with an amalgam of mercury and used for the gilding of brass. This mixture was applied very thinly, particularly by the Victorians, and a surfeit of enthusiasm when cleaning such pieces is certain to result in the removal of the gilded finish, leaving plain brass on the furniture and gold on the cleaning material.

LATE 19th CENTURY WRITING TABLE

THIS writing table dates from about 1890 and was probably made by a firm such as Cribb & Co. of Leeds who specialised in reproducing Hepplewhite and other late 18th century designs during the revival which occurred towards the end of the reign of Queen Victoria.

Usually of mahogany, though occasionally of satinwood, these tables had square, tapering legs with spade feet

Late 19th century writing table £90

and boxwood stringing on the edges. The two short drawers were furnished with brass loop handles and the leather covered top was typically surmounted by a pair of sloping shoulder pieces fitted for inkwells and pens.

These tables are usually well made and worth buying, though it is quite easy to adapt an inlaid Edwardian dressing table.

Simply remove the mirror and slightly alter the superstructure to suit your particular taste. If you are not experienced with tools, this need not deter you from the attempt for it is really very simple; even the job of fitting a leather cover on the surface can be undertaken by anyone.

The leather need not be fully inserted into the top of the table, but the edges should be flush in order that they do not get lifted with use. Score a line with a Stanley knife about one inch from the edge of the table top and carefully chamfer the wood inside the

line to the depth of your piece of leather. Cut your leather about half an inch larger all round than the finished size and stick it with a contact adhesive. Finally, trim the leather carefully with a sharp blade and press it well into the chamfer, hard against the straight line originally scored.

KNEEHOLE DESK CIRCA 1695

KNEEHOLE desks were originally designed for use as dressing tables and are basically, chests of drawers with recesses cut to accommodate the knees of persons seated before the mirror which stood on top.

It soon became apparent, however, that they made ideal writing tables and they stayed as dual purpose pieces of furniture until the latter half of the 18th century.

This particularly fine example comes from the William and Mary period and is made of walnut with ebony arabesque marquetry panels. These are inlays of floral and geometric scrolls, usually found within a simple, rectangular frame.

Kneehole desk, circa 1695 £750

This desk rests upon small bun feet typical of the period and has a recessed cupboard with a small drawer in the apron above. The drawers are made of oak and have dust boards fitted between them.

You cannot really pick and choose when buying a desk of this type and period—they are rare, especially those having a recessed slide set between the top and first drawer.

A Georgian kneehole desk lacquered in the Chinese style with a recessed cupboard, frieze drawer and bracket feet. £400

VICTORIAN
OAK PEDESTAL DESK

ALTHOUGH the kneehole desk with a centre cupboard was still popular in the mid 18th century, the style developed somewhat to incorporate two pedestals, each having three or four drawers, surmounted by a flat table top which itself contained two or three drawers.

At first these were made as single units, often double sided to stand in the centre of a room, and soon became extremely popular in libraries. They were, however, rather large and cumbersome in this form and later models were made in three sections to facilitate removal and installation.

Victorian oak pedestal desk £55

Pedestal desks date from about 1750 until the end of the 19th century and the difficulty in pricing them stems from the fact that the style changed hardly at all during that time.

There are general pointers to dating pieces, such as the depth of polish and general construction but it is really only after gaining experience by handling furniture for some time that you will develop that sixth sense which tells you that a piece is genuine.

VICTORIAN
CYLINDER TOP DESK

A DESIGN like this could never have come from any period but the Victorian. It is made of mahogany and has a cylindrical cover for the writing drawer which slides up and back into the body of the desk to reveal pigeon holes and small drawers. The leather covered writing surface pulls forward from beneath the pigeon hole section, and this invariably has an adjustable centre piece and a well for storing paper and envelopes.

Almost large enough to live in, this is an extremely solidly built piece of furniture and ideal for use as a small office by one man or one woman businesses, since there is ample room for storage of ledgers and all the miscellanea of paper which is attendant on any commercial or literary enterprise.

The cylinder is made by glueing strips of pine or mahogany edge to edge round a former; when dry the wood is sanded to a smooth shape, veneered and polished. This process is quite satisfactory provided the desk has not been kept in a damp environment, when the cylinder is certain to warp and, once this has happened, repair is virtually impossible. If you should find one in this state, no matter how good the condition of the rest of the desk, harden your heart and ignore it unless you are prepared to afford the high cost of having a new cylinder specially made.

Victorian cylinder top desk £60

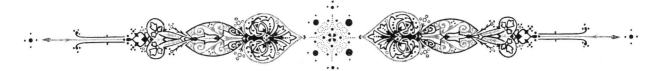

Sofas

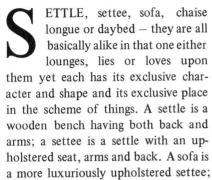

SETTLE, settee, sofa, chaise longue or daybed — they are all basically alike in that one either lounges, lies or loves upon them yet each has its exclusive character and shape and its exclusive place in the scheme of things. A settle is a wooden bench having both back and arms; a settee is a settle with an upholstered seat, arms and back. A sofa is a more luxuriously upholstered settee; a couch, a luxurious sofa, although more suitable for reclining than sitting on. A chaise longue is a daybed with the addition of an armrest; and a daybed, as the name suggests, is a most useful piece of furniture to have around when overtaken by the urge to indulge in forty winks in the daytime — as opposed to a night bed — if you see what I mean!

CHIPPENDALE STYLE SETTEE

IN the three editions of the *Gentleman and Cabinet Maker's Director* which Chippendale published in 1754, 1759 and 1762 can be seen adaptations of just about every conceivable fashion from baroque to rococo, from Chinese to Gothic and back again. This may well have increased Mr. Chippendale's income but it has made life somewhat confusing for inexperienced antique collectors and dealers of the 20th century who tend to link his name primarily with a particular style of dining chair.

The mahogany framed, Chippendale style settee illustrated below, for example, has, at first glance, little in common with his ribbon back dining chairs with their cabriole legs and fine carving. Nevertheless, the beautiful proportions and indefinable sense of style in the square legs, the placing of the stretcher and the upright scroll arms, quite definitely bear the mark of the master designer's hand.

Chippendale style settee £275

This style of settee is usually large – at least a three, often four or even five seater – so it will need a fairly large room if it is to be seen and appreciated to the best advantage.

Owing to the immense popularity of Chippendale's designs, his influence can often be detected in furniture produced all over Europe and in the widespread British Colonies that were. It cannot, therefore, be stressed too strongly that the vast majority of "Chippendale" pieces are made from his designs only and although many, like this settee, bear the mark of his genius, only relatively few items of furniture exist which were actually made in his own workshops, these being generally of his more sophisticated styles.

LATE 18th CENTURY SETTEE

HERE is another large settee from the last quarter of the 18th century in which can be seen the influence of both Sheraton and Hepplewhite, with perhaps a touch of the Robert Adams.

While the general style and proportions reflect the slender delicacy of Sheraton and Hepplewhite, the use of satinwood inlay on the top and front rails follows the trend set by Robert Adam of using mahogany for the basic frame with more exotic woods employed as decorative inlays.

Late 18th century settee £375

Although this is a large settee, the wide seat and finely turned legs achieve the standard of classical elegance for which the late 18th century is renowned.

It was this insistence on classical correctness, however, which eventually caused a decline in the popularity of these beautiful pieces – people came to consider them simply vehicles for the designer's creative urges, feeling that comfort, warmth and practicality were being neglected in the search for perfection of style.

DUCHESSE

THE original French version of the duchesse was a large, tub-shaped chair with a matching stool which were designed in such a way that when placed together they formed a daybed.

Both Sheraton and Hepplewhite were quick to recognise the potential of this piece of furniture, introducing it to their English customers in the

The Egyptian Room at Brighton's Royal Pavillion.

1770s, in the form of a pair of tub shaped chairs (one often larger than the the other) with a matching stool between. Hepplewhite's suggestion was that it should be placed in the anteroom — doubtless so that the 18th century hostess prone to attacks of the vapours could lie down to compose herself without having to trudge up flights of stairs to the nearest bedroom.

Having been made in three separate units, few duchesses have survived intact (there must be a joke there somewhere) and, complete, they command rather high prices on account of their rarity value. They are extremely useful pieces of furniture, however, for they can be used separately until the extra guest arrives for an overnight stay when all other beds are taken.

REGENCY COUCH

THERE are a number of Regency couches, all of which are influenced by the styles of Egypt, Rome or early Greece.

It was Sheraton in his *Cabinet Dictionary* who first introduced a couch of this style to England and its scroll ends and lion's paw feet made it one of the most elegant fashions to have been seen at that time. Inevitably, the style became popular and exerted considerable influence, not only on the furniture of the period but on the whole conduct of domestic life in that it seemed to embody the spirit of Gracious Living which large portions of the population were striving to achieve.

This Regency couch is made of either mahogany or rosewood and better examples are enhanced by the use of brass string inlay or elaborate

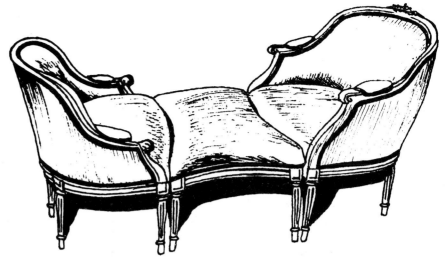

Duchesse £450

scrollwork on the front and back rails. The curving lines of arms and back are in the best Regency tradition, as are the sabre legs and the brass claw castors with which they are embellished.

An excellent couch this, which must be covered in a Regency stripe material and finished off with bolster cushions.

Do-it-yourself upholsterers may wonder how the fabric is fixed along the inside of the seat and bottom of the back. Two screws will be seen at the rear of the piece, fastening the back to the arms and when these are removed the back may be carefully pulled from the main frame, where it is held in place by a number of dowel pegs.

Once the back is taken off, the task of upholstering becomes quite straightforward and, providing that the dowels have not been broken, the couch will go together again securely and easily.

REGENCY DAYBED

DAYBEDS have been in England since about the time of William Shakespeare, when they were inclined to be rather primitively made of a palliasse supported on webbing stretched over a bed frame. This was normally equipped with a panelled headboard but, by standards set during later periods, the piece was rather unattractive and remarkably uncomfortable.

The flamboyance of the Charles II period demanded that the daybed's appearance, at least, should be tarted up somewhat and saw the introduction of canework panels and splendidly carved walnut frames. It was during the Regency period, however, that the piece

Regency daybed £140

really came into its own. No longer was the daybed simply something to flop on to; the fine flowing lines of the scroll ends and sabre legs demanded a similar degree of elegant decadence from the disposition of the limbs of any who reclined upon it and this, combined with the relative comfort of the upholstery made it the ideal setting for the start of a seduction

The gentlemen of the 19th century would have bought a daybed of this style with only one thing in mind. So, I suspect, will the gentlemen of the late 20th century!

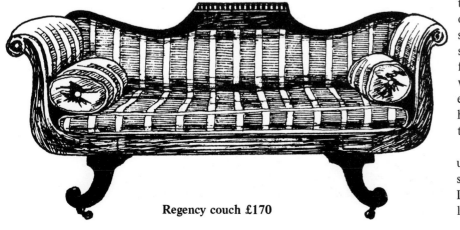

Regency couch £170

GRECIAN COUCH

THIS couch is from the William IV period and shows how the sensuous flow of line, typical of the Regency styles, gave way to the more formal, stiff-backed fashions which were to follow.

It was Michelangelo Nicholson in *The Practical Cabinet Maker, Upholsterer and Complete Decorator* of 1826 who first suggested the use of short, stumpy legs to replace the flowing sabre legs of the Regency period, and it is surprising how these, together with a slight tightening of the curves which form the arms, can so alter the character of a piece of furniture.

Couches in this style are usually to be found made of mahogany and this particular example is decorated with some ebony inlay.

Grecian couch £150

The more formal masculinity of this piece demands a stronger looking upholstery material than Regency stripe and it is best covered in leather, buttoned on the back and carried straight over the scroll arms. The palliasse seat should be studded and bolster cushions of perfectly cylindrical shape add the finishing touch.

VICTORIAN CHAISE LONGUE

AS the rococo style began to gain momentum in about 1830, following its adoption in the interiors of Crockfords and Apsley House, London, it was still rather inhibited by the restrained period of classical correctness which it superseded.

The death of William IV and the beginning of the reign of a beautiful young queen soon gave added impetus to the movement and, for a number of years, the freshly frivolous styles of the early Victorian period were to be seen in all the more fashionable houses of London and the provinces.

This couch, from the beginning of that period, would have been considered the last word in levity of design with its turned legs and exaggerated curves, not to mention the suggestion of carving on the back, which, as the style progressed, was to develop into something approaching an art form in its own right.

Victorian chaise longue £85

Furniture of this period can be bought at reasonable prices, by virtue of the fact that it does not fall clearly into any particular style and is, therefore, not so pleasing to eyes accustomed to the definite characteristics which typify the pieces of the major periods.

This chaise longue has a mahogany or walnut frame (though a few are to be found with rosewood frames) and brass cup castors terminate the short, turned legs. Although it is slightly heavy in appearance, this can be alleviated by deep buttoning the end and back. Good quality velvet is probably the best material to use when recovering one of these pieces, though they will accept a surprisingly wide range of other materials quite well.

EARLY VICTORIAN SOFA

THIS sofa, from the same period as the turned leg chaise longue previously illustrated, again demonstrates the first timorous steps from the classical to the rococo taken by cabinet makers and designers of the period; the basic style is still Grecian but they could not resist the temptation to try their hands at French rococo carving and embellishment.

Unfortunately, the British craftsmen were relatively inexperienced in the art of rococo carving and many of their attempts at capturing the flowing exuberance of the French, Louis XIV style were extremely amateurish.

This piece, too, is large and heavy-looking, with a mahogany or pale walnut frame and I never liked the style until I saw one which had been bleached almost white, covered in a Regency stripe material and given tassels on the bolster cushions.

Although I am not particularly in favour of tampering with early furniture I must admit that there is occasionally a very good case to be made for the practice, especially when it gives a new lease of life to an otherwise rather unattractive item.

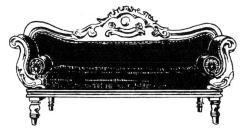

Early Victorian sofa £65

DRAWING ROOM SOFA

BY the time this sofa came along, in 1850, the craftsmen were beginning to understand what it was that they had for so long been trying to achieve.

In this happy blend of both cabinet maker's and upholsterer's arts, the Greek and Roman influences have fully disappeared and the intricate buttoning of the upholstery is calculated to emphasise the soft comfort of the piece, while this and the pierced carving round the medallion back alleviate the tendency toward heaviness which might otherwise have detracted from the overall effect.

The exposed part of the frame deserves attention for, apart from the fine scrollwork, there is a nicely carved cluster of roses atop the medallion back; and the legs, having lost the dullness of the earlier plain turning, are well proportioned to give the whole piece a better line than Victorian furniture had hitherto achieved.

All in all, this is a nicely designed sofa; it is pleasing to the eye, very well made and comfortable—could anyone ask for more?

Drawing room sofa £155

VICTORIAN SOFA

THIS beautiful couch, with its exuberantly deep buttoned back and seat is now, I am pleased to say, getting all the attention it so rightly deserves. The walnut frame is finely carved to emphasise the swooping lines and the delightfully exaggerated cabriole legs convey the impression that they are going to start skipping about the room the moment no one is watching.

Like a good piece of sculpture, this is one of those items of furniture which not only delights the eye but demands to be touched and I find it difficult to

believe that, in past years, dustmen were paid to cart them off to the corporation tip like plague victims when no one was looking.

Which reminds me that when I first began dealing in antiques I spotted a beautiful little chair of the same style as this sofa perched on the local dust-cart.

Giving chase, I flagged the driver down and, although he doubted my sanity, persuaded him to exchange the chair for a pound note, my address and the promise that I would pay a similar amount for any other such pieces he

might come across.

For about six months or so I did very well from this source despite the fact that my neighbours considered me more than suspect as a steady stream of dustcarts called to deliver more rubbish than they ever removed.

Gone, alas, are such days—your up to date dustman knows more about the values of antiques than many a collector and is liable to charge higher prices for his wares than the average West End showroom, even though he probably charges more to take stuff away than he used to.

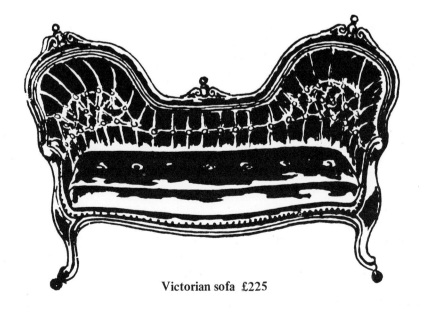

Victorian sofa £225

LOUIS XV STYLE SETTEE

BY the last quarter of the 19th century, successful artistic inventiveness seemed to have run out of steam and furniture manufacturers were having to leaf through old, half forgotten fashions in order to tempt their customers.

Out of the ensuing wealth of reproductions there arose a great demand for Chippendale, Sheraton and Hepplewhite style furniture as well as for the gilt elegance of the Louis XV period of which this little settee is an example.

The original, 18th century pieces, of course, command very high prices indeed but this delicate reproduction, which has all the attributes responsible for the style's success 150 years earlier, will fetch only a fraction of this figure.

It is beautifully made with carved French cabriole legs, undulating arm supports and a nicely framed back which harmonises gracefully with the seat rail.

Louis XV style settee £155

These settees need (as do chairs of similar style) to be covered in a tapestry material finished with a toning gimp.

If the gilding is a little rubbed and in need of refurbishing, gilt paste can be bought in varying shades at a cost of about £1 and it can be applied with a rag. If in doubt as to the precise shade, go for a slightly lighter colour and, when dry, dab over it with a little walnut stain until the correct colour is obtained; this will have the added advantage of apparently ageing the new gilt as the stain tends to lodge in the gullies, making these slightly darker than the surrounding higher areas.

VICTORIAN SOFA

HERE is another sofa from the same period as the one before last, again incorporating much that is best of Victorian rococo.

The piece, well proportioned despite the flamboyance of the back, has a particularly good front rail, carved in the centre and flowing beautifully into the carved cabriole legs which, in turn, sweep nicely up into the scrolled arms.

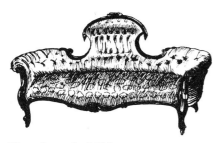

Victorian sofa £210

50

Years ago, I received a telephone call from a woman inviting me to see a sofa, which, according to her description, was identical to this one and which she was considering selling.

Arriving at her address, I was greeted by a positive cartoon of a woman—low slung bosom, lorgnette and miniature dog clasped underarm—who looked me up and down, and demanded that I keep my voice to a whisper so as not to upset Ming (the underarm dog). The woman told me that the sofa belonged to Ming and she could only part with it if Ming approved the sale.

We eventually arrived at a parlour in the centre of which, to my astonishment, was a couch exactly similar to the one illustrated here; exactly the same, that is apart from the legs which had been crudely sawn off just below the spot where they joined the front and back rails. Before I could say anything more than "The legs . . ." Madame confided in reverent tones that she had had to have the legs shortened so that Ming could get on and off his bed unaided, the little darling had not been able to manage the task alone and he had been so fond of the sofa that she felt she had no choice...

Although I am fond of dogs, I am afraid that, personally, I would have had the little darling's legs lengthened rather than spoil such a lovely piece. I did not buy the sofa.

UPHOLSTERED CHAISE LONGUE

UNTIL the decline of the Regency period, the upholsterer played a very minor role in the production of home furnishings and was really not in the same league as the cabinet maker, his work consisting mainly of hanging curtains and tapestries and lining walls with material.

Around the 1840s, however, there was a small, bloodless revolution within the furniture factories, the upholsterer rising to hitherto unheard of heights in his craft, virtually dictating the shape and style of chairs and settees and leaving the cabinet maker only the responsibility for making relatively simple frames of birch or ash.

This chaise longue is typical of the period and is similar to many of those illustrated by H. Lawford in his *Book of Designs,* most of which reveal no timber at all in their finished state. In order to show the buttoning to advantage, while retaining the warm voluptuousness of the piece, a chaise longue of this kind should always be covered in velvet, bearing in mind that the better quality velvets are less liable to the unsightly flattening of the nap which commonly occurs with the cheaper varieties.

Upholstered chaise longue £95

If you would like a deep buttoned chaise longue but can only find one which has been covered straight over, do not despair—it is a simple job to have the holes made which will make deep buttoning possible.

When measuring up in order to determine the length of material required, simply lay a tape measure over the length and add one and a half inches for each button in the path of the tape, repeating the process for the width.

CHESTERFIELD

THE late 19th century saw a spate of fatly upholstered chairs and couches and this, named after the 19th Earl of Chesterfield, represents the art of upholstery at its peak.

For some reason, the deep buttoned, leather covered Chesterfield has become accepted as a symbol of its proud owner's having arrived. Certainly they are not cheap, particularly when well upholstered in deep buttoned leather, though bought "as is" a Chesterfield in a fairly tatty state of upholstery need not prove too expensive and might well be a good investment.

The Chesterfield is widely regarded within the upholstery trade as being one of the trickiest things to cover, particularly in good quality leather. For this reason, taking a full two weeks of a professional's time, Chesterfields simply have to be expensive if they are in good condition.

It is possible, of course, for a competent amateur upholsterer to make a very workmanlike job but it is not a task which should be undertaken by someone without considerable experience of this kind of work. Once the art of deep buttoning has been mastered, the bulk of the task should prove pretty straight forward but the difficulty comes as the corner is turned between the back and the arm. Here, unless great care is excercised the material will tend to gather in over-abundance at the bottom leaving none at the top to be carried over the curve and fixed on the underside of the arm.

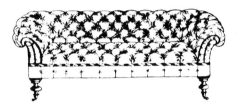

Chesterfield £50

I have seen Chesterfields fitted very nicely with loose covers and these are quite acceptable as a second best—perhaps while the owners stuff their pound notes into the body of the piece against the day they decide to have the job done properly.

OTTOMAN

THE ottoman derives from the Turkish Empire of the same name and reflects the early 18th century interest in the exotic East.

It was, in its original state, a low, stuffed seat having neither arms nor back but, after the variations in style shown at the Great Exhibition of 1851, any cushioned seat made to accommodate several persons sitting with their backs to one another was accepted as an ottoman. There are some varieties consisting of three or four separate units which are locked together by

Ottoman £260

means of brass catches.

Illustrated is a particularly fine Victorian example having a carved walnut frame, cabriole legs and a cluster of finely carved roses on the top of the centre section. The deep buttoned velvet seat looks particularly attractive provided someone is prepared to devote time to removing the dust which collects in the wells.

Space is essential for a piece of furniture such as this, for in a small room, there will be room for little else and conversation rarely flows between people sitting back to back facing mute walls.

Generally speaking, reupholstery of these pieces is a job best left to professionals but, if you must attempt it yourself, watch out for the centre-piece! All faces of this section have to be buttoned simultaneously if the

proper effect is to be achieved and the tension on the buttons obtained by pulling on those in opposite faces.

LATE 19th CENTURY INLAID COUCH

THIS nice little Edwardian couch is made of mahogany with boxwood string inlay. The design reflects a strong 18th century influence, particularly in the finely turned arm supports and the Hepplewhite, square tapered legs and spade feet yet, despite this, the piece manages to achieve a style of its own which is at once delicate yet practical.

The better examples will be found to have bone and ivory inlay work on the back and the front rail and, although couches of this style are not designed for an evening's lolling in front of the television, they are good

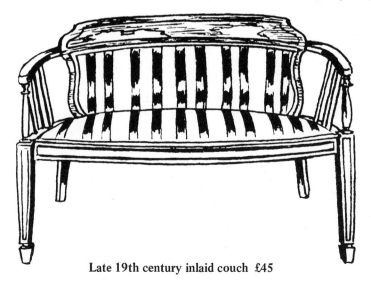

Late 19th century inlaid couch £45

value for money and make quite nice perches for ladies who enjoy the civilised delicacy of afternoon tea.

Cover these Edwardian couches straight over—they are far too finely framed to support a heavy-looking deep buttoned effect—but be warned; they are almost always too long to allow either back or seat to be covered from a single width of material. For this reason, they are probably best covered in a striped material with the seam concealed along the edge of the stripe for, unless the very best quality velvet is used (and velvet is really correct for this style) it will tend to mark if it is used to recover a seat on the cross.

LATE 19th CENTURY SETTEE

THIS one would never have won a prize for elegance but it is cheap and functional and, with a little care, can be made to look loved and at home in most surroundings.

The frame is normally of mahogany, though it may be of beech either ebonised or stained to simulate mahogany. The legs give some indication of the quality of manufacture of the piece since, as a rule, finer turned legs were produced by the better manufacturers but, unfortunately, even the very best of these couches is not very good.

It would perhaps be as well to mention that, in this context, the word good is used more in the sense of desirability of style than in that of sturdiness and quality of structural manufacture. Many "good" antiques may, indeed, be found to be extremely fragile, and quite unserviceable as pieces of furniture while others, such as this couch, may be extremely functional and very serviceable but sadly lacking charm, elegance or style.

Late 19th century settee £40

Usually found in the company of a pair of matching armchairs, a couch such as this can be improved by finely buttoning the upholstery along the top of the back and studding that of the arms; this has the effect of drawing the eye away from the rather dreary frame.

Always look under the seat before spending money on one of these since sagging springs and worn webbing indicate an imminent repair bill which is just not worth it.

EDWARDIAN MAHOGANY COUCH

Edwardian mahogany couch £25

THIS is what your grandmother, as a blushing young bride, will most probably have furnished her lounge with—your actual modern couch, pre First World War style. What more could a young wife have asked of life in those happy, pre-suffragette days than to recline on this, winding up the family phonograph and sucking scented cachous?

This, surely one of the last pieces made to aspire to the title of antique in the future, is a conglomeration of styles dreamed up by a works designer of doubtful talent whose chief value lay in his ability to adapt an existing style to the skills and machinery available in his factory in such a manner as to minimise wastage of time and timber. If he could throw in the occasional innovation of his own, so much the better, since this would give his designs a degree of originality while satisfying his creative urges in as harmless a way as possible.

Invariably given a mahogany frame by dependable manufacturers, couches to this general design have usually lasted quite well even though most

other furniture produced at about the same time has long since fallen by the wayside.

Cover one of these in just about anything that goes with the wallpaper, possibly buttoning the back to add a little status to the appearance of the piece.

SETTLE

THIS is one of the earliest forms of English purpose built seating and is a direct descendant of the plain bench seat which was fixed to the wall panelling in mediaeval upper class houses.

Most settles have panelled backs, which give them the appearance of only recently having been sawn out of the wall of the ancestral home, and they are equipped with arms and a hinged seat which, open, reveals a very

WILLIAM AND MARY ROOM

Dating from the late seventeenth century the furniture in this room shows a marked change of style from that of the Elizabethan and Stuart periods of the previous century.

There is a new sense of delicacy and sophistication in the pad and Spanish feet of the stool and lacquered dressing table, and even the country-made spinning wheel has some nicely turned decoration.

The corner cupboard with its shaped shelves, contains a selection of early Delftware and there is an interesting pony skin trunk on the window seat to the right of the picture.

(Courtesy Geffrye Museum)

useful storage space. This latter feature cannot fail to appeal to families with children, when it will serve as a toy box, and to those wives whose husbands phone to say they will be bringing the boss home in half an hour on the one day of the year that the place is looking like the Isle of Wight after a pop festival.

The style of the settle has changed little over the years and it was the traditional furniture of farmhouses and inns of the 18th century. Usually made of oak or elm, or a combination of the two, the best will have mellowed to a beautiful honey colour with a rich, deep polish.

The large, plump cushions which go so well with a piece of this kind can be covered in virtually any material and the high back will be found very useful in draughty houses.

Settle £95

Settles may often be found to contain a certain amount of worm, but, unless the piece is absolutely riddled, this need not detract from its value, but to be safe, treat every hole with a reputable preparation.

Check also the hinges and arms for excessive damage, particularly the latter, since repairs will possibly entail the use of new wood which will stand out like a sore thumb unless it is carefully stained to simulate the colour of age.

BACON CUPBOARD

SETTLES were occasionally produced with a very high back and a canopy to give a comfortable, womb-like sense of security to the sitter.

Bacon cupboard £115

These, usually country made, later developed into quite large pieces like the one illustrated and were used as store cupboards for food and hanging places for sides of bacon.

Following the style of the settle, the seat section was hinged to provide extra storage space though the front of the base was often provided with dummy drawer fronts—the 18th century farmhouse equivalent of plastic beam one-upmanship.

Like the settle, bacon cupboards were generally made of oak, elm or a combination of the two and, accordingly, show some beautiful variations of grain which are emphasised by the deep shine of years of polishing.

According to early inventories it was the practice to position the settle at the end of the bed, particularly in smaller houses, consisting as many did of only one large, general purpose room. This gave a degree of privacy to any one who retired early while providing seating for others who might wish to burn the midnight oil.

As the settle developed into the bacon cupboard, still at the end of the bed, it could well provide the Darwinian link between primitive man's nocturnal foraging habits and those of his refrigerator-raiding, 20th century descendants.

WROUGHT IRON GARDEN BENCH

THIS is a particularly fine iron garden seat of the kind so beloved by the Victorians.

In their enthusiasm for the new techniques opened up by the rapid technological advances of their time they delighted in the exploitation of the materials available to them and the new uses to which they could be put. Monuments and buildings reflected the desire to overcome the transience of the natural lifespan and it was only to be expected that rustic looking benches, tables, chairs and stands should be made, not of perishable wood, but of iron fashioned to represent it in its natural state.

Originally intended for the garden, furniture of this kind adopts a totally new dimension when it is brought indoors, and is sometimes used to advantage in a room which opens on to the garden, though there is probably no reason why it should not be used in a flat halfway up a high rise block.

Wrought iron garden bench £110

A regular coat of paint is all the renovation iron furniture needs and, with the addition of a few cushions, benches such as this can be made to look very attractive—and not nearly so uncomfortable as their appearance suggests.

The example illustrated, made to resemble the fruits of a day's labour in Epping Forest, is one of the better pieces of its type and therefore on the expensive side but it should not be too difficult to find an old park or railway bench in a scrap yard or dealer's shed. All that these usually need is a coat of paint and some new planks to make them extremely acceptable pieces of furniture and good conversation pieces, too, particularly if they bear the monogram of the railway company or park.

 # Bookcases

RECENTLY, a leaflet came into my possession. It was printed for Her Majesty's Stationery Office and is packed with gems of easy-to-read, good-heaven's-above-I-didn't-know-that kind of statistical information about the British book industry and the book buying and borrowing habits of the British public.

Like many people, I can never resist an opportunity to pass on information of this sort, particularly if some kind of pretext can be manufactured to make it

relevant, and have no hesitation in doing so here. William Caxton, who was born in Kent in 1422, settled for a time in Bruges where he learned the art of printing. On returning to his native shores, he set up a press in Westminster and, in 1477, issued his *Dictes and Sayings of the Philosyphres,* the first book printed in England.

Since that time, the British book industry has grown somewhat and, despite those prophets of doom who at various times have forecast that the development of radio, films, television and the gramaphone would each sound the death knell of the book business, there has been an incredible increase in the production of the printed word.

Consider, if you will — between 1938 and 1971 there were as many books published in Britain as there had been throughout the previous five centuries. In 1971, nearly 33,000 titles were published in Britain alone and, although

models up to four feet six inches high and with proportionately increased girth.

The great drawback with revolving bookcases lies in their unique virtue — the swivel action. No one, but no one, seems able to resist giving them a flick in passing and, unless the books are jammed in tightly, or otherwise anchored, the effect of such treatment resembles that of some of the more ingenious anti-personnel weapons currently being produced - a hail of lethal volumes are projected in all horizontal directions simultaneously with a velocity calculated to cause considerable hurt to anyone in the immediate vicinity.

the British buy, on average, only four books per household per year, we now borrow, on average, 38 books per household. This all adds up to a lot of books, a lot of reading and the need for quite a few miles of storage space. Faced with a grim picture of all these households buying and borrowing books at the rate of 42 volumes per year, I felt that the least I could do would be to suggest a few bookcases, shelves and magazine racks to house them.

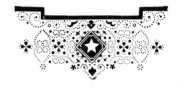

Revolving bookcase (plain) £40
Revolving bookcase (inlaid) £55

REVOLVING BOOKCASE

THE revolving bookcase is the ideal piece of furniture for the idle bibliophile or for the family which lacks the wall space necessary for the more conventional methods of book display and storage.

Made in significant quantities between 1880 and 1920, many were given as free gifts by fast talking sales representatives, who offered them as inducements to potential purchasers of the innumerable home educator or encyclopaedia volumes which were in vogue at the time. They were made in two qualities, plain or inlaid, and in two sizes; standard or large, and in these days, the standard size, inlaid, revolving bookcase is the one most likely to fetch the highest price. Most were made about three feet high but I have seen larger

CANTERBURY

LIKE so many other pieces of furniture the canterbury is so called, not for any mystical trade reason, but after the name of the first important person to order it from the designer's catalogue (though nowadays names are bestowed for far more Freudian reasons).

Originally designed to hold sheet music, this particular item could just as well have been called the Archbishop since, according to Sheraton, it was named after the Archbishop of Canterbury, who was among the first to place an order for one. Most of the original, late 18th century, varieties were rectangular in shape and were made with a drawer in the base (doubtless for the storage of less popular pieces of music). Castors enabled them to be pushed beneath the piano and the two or three partitions in the upper section were usually dipped in the middle to allow easy removal of the sheets of music.

Following the inventions of Messrs. Edison, Marconi and Baird, the taste for home-produced music has dwindled sadly but, fortunately, the bulk of Sunday newspapers and the increase in magazines of quality has ensured the continuing usefulness of these delightful pieces of furniture.

Top left: Regency canterbury £85
Top right: Victorian canterbury £50
Centre: late 18th century canterbury
£135

Earlier examples of these are the most expensive, though those of mahogany are not too dear as a rule, and satinwood pieces can fetch insanely high prices, one recently selling for £750!

Regency canterburys are of mahogany or rosewood; the later Victorian examples are generally of burr walnut with flamboyantly fretted partitions or barley twist supports.

BRASS MAGAZINE STAND

THE first half of the 19th century saw a profusion of brass objects from cake stands to fire irons and from standard lamps to magazine stands. All were of good quality and all worth the money they fetch today.

Brass magazine stand, left £55
Brass magazine stand, right £40

Standing on a tripod of tubular brass, the magazine stands generally have three brass grille partitions, mounted on an oak base. The centre partition was usually made higher than the other two in order that the stand could be easily lifted and transported about the room and the better examples have paw feet and scenic views pressed into the brass outer partitions.

Owing to the development of good hard wearing lacquers, brass has ceased to be the bane of the housewife's life since, if the lacquering is done properly, the brass beneath will remain clean and bright for an indefinite period.

For those who feel, as I do, that brass looks its best in its plain polished

state, the cleaning of these magazine racks is enormously simplified by virtue of the fact that the partitions are held in place by means of screws beneath the oak platform.

WHATNOT

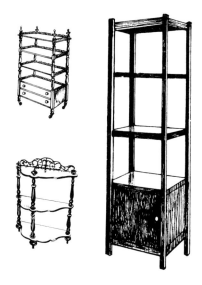

Regency whatnot (top left) £115
Victorian whatnot (bottom left) £60
Late 18th century whatnot (right) £140

FORMERLY of French design, the whatnot made its English debut in about 1790 and was enthusiastically received as the ideal display piece for books and bric a brac.

The earlier examples are generally of rather simple designs and usually of rosewood or mahogany. Subsequent styles, late Regency and Victorian, are often found to be quite elaborate with shaped shelves and fretwork galleries, while some of the Victorian whatnots were made to fit into a corner or enlarged up to four feet in length and designed to be placed against a wall.

The whatnot is one of those pieces which could have been called anything at all. The original French name was etagere, but this apparently taxed the memory or linguistic talents of our ancestors to the extent that they fell back on just the kind of name we would be likely to use today; thingamebob, oojah, whatsit, howsyerfarther, each would have served equally well.

Words such as these remind me of the morning last winter when I met a young Spanish buyer on his first trip to

Britain. He greeted me with the word "Hotinit" and I, knowing virtually no Spanish, assumed this to be an equivalent of "Good morning" or "How do you do". In the spirit of international friendliness, I returned the greeting.

It was only during later conversation that I learned that he had been using what he thought to be the usual English phrase of greeting, having heard so many English tourists use it to each other while strolling through the streets of the Costa Brava holiday towns.

HANGING SHELVES

HANGING shelves have been used since the 16th century when they were constructed in the form of a simple square, generally quite small, bisected by a single shelf and thus providing three usable surfaces.

During the 17th century they tended to become rather wider than their height, often sporting elaborate cornices and carved decoration and usually with a lip along the front edge of each shelf to prevent plates and other displayed pieces from falling off.

Regency hanging shelves (top left) £45
Victorian hanging shelves (top right)
£20
Regency hanging shelves (centre) £50

It was Chippendale, in the third edition of his *Director*, which was published in 1762, who designed hanging shelves specifically for books and, al-

though these were usually plainer than those intended to display china, they proved extremely popular throughout the later years of the 18th century and during the Regency period.

Some of the best hanging shelves ever made appeared in George Smith's *Collection of Designs for Household Furniture and Interior Decoration*, which was published in 1808, many having graduated shelves with brass edging and elaborate scroll supports of rosewood or mahogany or sometimes, with brass, lyre-shaped supports.

REGENCY BOOKSHELVES

THERE were a number of free standing bookshelves designed throughout the Regency period to enable books in current use to be more conveniently situated in the room than those displayed in the larger, wall type bookcases which predominated during that era.

They were made of either rosewood or mahogany and were usually embellished with brass grills, castors, or intricate inlay work, all of which makes them very attractive and, therefore rather expensive pieces particularly since they were quite rare owing to the fact that they are generally used only in large houses having separate libraries.

It was Sheraton, that arch enemy of women's lib, who emphasised that these bookshelves should be made light enough for ladies to move them from room to room but no one seems to have taken any notice of him for once (or else the ladies of the Regency period were not the delicate lilies they appeared).

The problem is that bookshelves of this kind seem to act as magnets for books and, when fully loaded, are so heavy that four female Russian shot putters would be hard put to it to move one more than a few inches at a time.

Regency bookshelves (left) £250
Regency bookshelves (right) £450

CHIFFONIER

THIS delightful piece first put in an appearance around 1800 when it achieved instant popularity.

It was designed, possibly as an alternative for the large sideboards of the period, or as a replacement for the commode, whose flowing lines and profuse decoration were not to the taste of the leaders of Regency fashion.

Regency chiffonier £300

Whatever its parentage, the chiffonier was made, often in pairs, with a glass fronted cabinet in the lower part and, usually, shelves above, which were frequently constructed with lyre or fine scroll shaped supports.

Earlier pieces were made usually of rosewood and, occasionally, of satinwood, while those of later manufacture

Early nineteenth century, mahogany bookcase

after a design in Sheraton's Encyclopaedia, 1806.

were of either of those woods and mahogany.

The piece illustrated has features which clearly suggest a late Regency style, notably the brass mounted columns on either side of the glazed doors, the brass inlay on the frieze and the brass gallery round the topmost shelf.

Earlier examples are often found to have brass grilles backed by silk in the panelled doors, and the Victorians not uncommonly removed these, putting in glass as a means of providing more display space for their smaller treasures. A chiffonier which has been altered in this way can quite easily be restored to its former state with the grille from a damaged brass fireguard of suitable size being used to replace the glass. Indeed, it is always worth buying these large brass fireguards purely for the sake of the grilles, for although this material is available for purchase by the square foot, it is often very expensive.

GEORGIAN BOOKSHELF

THERE were any number of open bookshelves designed at the end of the 18th century and such is their practicality that they have remained popular ever since.

The Georgian variety, although elegantly tall and narrow with nicely graduated shelves, have always seemed to me to cost far more than they should. They are made of mahogany, rosewood

Georgian bookshelf £175

or satinwood, often japanned black or green and decorated with painted scenes or brass inlay. Some have cupboards or drawers in the base and they are supported on a variety of feet: bracket, scroll, claw, turned or with a shaped apron.

All these bookshelves are expensive, regardless of style, and as such are going to appeal more to the small investor than the family in search of pleasant furniture at reasonable prices.

If you fall into the latter category, I would strongly advise a bookshelf of the Edwardian variety, also illustrated above, as being attractively and well made of mahogany and usually priced at under £20

VICTORIAN OAK BOOKSHELVES

VICTORIAN bookshelves were, as a rule, much larger than those of previous periods and this was not so much as a result of a book buying boom as the Victorians' almost obsessive dislike of waste; hating to throw anything away, they needed a bookcase large enough to accommodate their own literary works as well as those of their forbears.

This is a typical Victorian oak bookcase, smothered with Elizabethan style carving in high relief and accommodating two useful cupboards in the base. The shelves, with true Victorian ingenuity, are for the first time, adjustable.

Victorian oak bookshelves £85

Bookcases like this are ideal for fairly large roomed houses, particularly if the inhabitants believe, as the Victorians did, that walls are there primarily to be concealed behind furniture and pictures.

It is a sad fact that, owing to the limited size of modern houses, pieces such as this are fast disappearing, being frequently broken up for the very fine carvings with which they were decorated, often representing fruit, grape vines and, occasionally, game birds and animal heads.

CHIPPENDALE BOOKCASE

MOST of the bookcases illustrated so far have been small enough to fit unobtrusively into the average room. We now move onto the larger fellows who need a little more thought on the part of prospective buyers.

The great difficulty with large pieces of furniture is their unavoidable tendency to dominate the room for better or worse, and although, in my opinion, a room needs furniture of varied height and proportion, it is essential that they complement each other in such a way that the apparent size of the largest piece is in no way obtrusive.

This nicely designed bookcase bears all the hallmarks of a Chippendale design, with the Gothic style glazed doors to the upper section and nicely panelled doors below. The delightful, fret cut, swan neck pediment came into fashion around 1760 and the central plinth between the swan necks was designed to support a portrait bust of some prominent person whose likeness might, it was hoped, exert a beneficial influence on the conduct of the household.

Chippendale was among the first designers to build bookcases as separate units and it is clear that the architectural feeling of existing designs had some influence on the manner in which his were styled, even to the churchy effect of the Gothic glazing bars in the upper set of doors. The dental cornice, too (below the pediment), is a feature of the architectural

embellishment, so named for its resemblance to teeth (though God help anyone with teeth like that) and the general feeling of the whole piece is that it might have been chipped out of a wall instead of standing against one.

Chippendale bookcase £390

REGENCY BOOKCASE

THIS nicely proportioned bookcase is from the Regency period and is made of rosewood with brass grilles to the panelled cupboard doors.

Regency bookcase £340

I once bought one of these in a rain-sodden condition from a gardening enthusiast who used it to display pot plants. Most of the veneer was curled

A small, early eighteenth century, dome-topped bureau cabinet veneered in walnut with a Vauxhall mirrored door and bracket feet.

VICTORIAN BOOKCASE

THIS is a typical Victorian bookcase, made in two parts, with glazed doors to the upper section and panelled cupboards to the lower, all shelves in both sections being adjustable for height.

The square corners suggest that this is an early Victorian piece, later designs tending to have rounded edges and a concave centre drawer front, beside being cheaper and less well made.

Earlier Victorian bookcases such as this were usually made of rosewood, mahogany or walnut and, because of their similarity to those of true Regency style, they are fairly easily converted to look more stylish by squaring off the upper corners of the doors and replacing the glass and wooden panels with brass grilles.

The ethics of this practice, however, are questionable, particularly since the piece might, at a later date, be foisted on some unsuspecting purchaser at the higher price commanded by a genuine Regency bookcase.

The only advice I can give to would-be purchasers is to look closely at the doors and the beading round the inside of the panels (which, if the job has not been properly done, might appear to be of newer wood) and, if you have any suspicions, hold on to your money.

The golden rule when buying antiques is to take note of your first

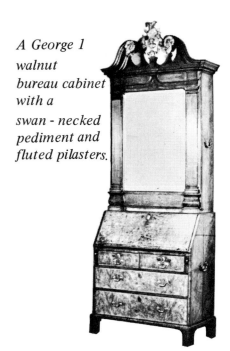

A George 1 walnut bureau cabinet with a swan-necked pediment and fluted pilasters.

reactions when seeing an article. These are usually correct and, with practice, a sixth sense can be developed which will warn you that something is wrong even though you might not be able to say precisely what it is.

GEORGIAN BUREAU BOOKCASE

THE introduction, at the end of the 17th century, of higher ceilings encouraged the development of taller items of furniture and one of the most successful adaptations of existing designs to the new fashion was the bureau bookcase which entailed quite simply the placing of a cabinet on top of the already popular sloping front bureau.

The earliest Queen Anne bureau cabinets had panelled doors to the upper section, often containing Vauxhall mirror glass, which enclosed a multitude of small drawers and pigeon holes. These can now be unbelievably expensive, those of good quality selling for over £5,000.

The main example illustrated is one of the earliest to be found in any quantity and it dates from the middle of the 18th century.

This design, usually made of mahogany or oak was initiated by Chippendale.

up like clocksprings, the door grilles had gone and, had it not been for the satisfaction I get from restoring nice pieces like this, I would not have bothered with it.

It took two weeks of frustration, neglected business and midnight oil to get the thing half finished, at which point I felt like giving up but could not afford to in view of the time spent on it already, so I spent a further two weeks trying to justify my investment.

Finally it was finished. It looked really beautiful in the house but, having earned virtually nothing for the past month, I had to sell it (even dealers have to eat). The first morning I displayed it in my shop, a Dutch dealer bought it and put it on his roofrack immediately, before seeing the rest of my stock (this was a sure sign that I had under-priced it). For almost an hour he nosed around, buying nothing else, before getting in his car and zooming away in search of further bargains.

As I stood in the street watching four weeks of hard labour disappear into the wide blue yonder, the blessed bookcase took off from the roof of the car with all the grace of a glider and demolished itself together with a section of someone's garden wall – mine! The man had forgotten, in his haste, to tie it down.

Victorian bookcase £65

60

Georgian bureau bookcase (left) £325
Queen Anne bureau bookcase (right) £5,500

Since bureau bookcase carcasses tend to be very similar, the pattern made by the glazing bars is a good aid to establishing the date of a piece. Unfortunately, however, it is not infallible, since many of the designs were used throughout the different periods.

Broadly, however, in the late 17th century, the glazing was of plain rectangles secured with putty behind substantial, half round mouldings. In the 1740s, the glass was mounted in a wavy frame and the establishment of mahogany soon after meant that, by the 1750s, the glazing bars could be finer and more decorative – usually forming 13 divisions, as illustrated above, or shaped in the fashion of Gothic church windows (see the Chippendale bookcase described on page 59)

HEPPLEWHITE STYLE BUREAU BOOKCASE

AT the end of the 18th century, Hepplewhite introduced diamond glazing and also flowing curves and polygonal shapes, often enriched with foliate designs, in the glazing of his furniture. Sheraton too, used similar forms, often enhanced by their superimpositions on pleated silks.

Original, 18th century, Hepplewhite bureau bookcases in exotic woods such as harewood can cost as much as £2,000 but, thankfully, his designs were extensively copied toward the

end of the following century and the illustrated example dates from this period.

This is an extremely elegant bookcase, extensively inlaid in various woods with bows, ribbons and garlands of flowers. Unlike most other bureau bookcases, it has four drawers, instead of the usual three, and the additional storage space thus created is another strong point in its favour. If I were recommending the month's star buy, this would surely be the one I would choose.

Most reproductions of this period are of plain mahogany enhanced with a boxwood string inlay and a conch shell in the centre of the bureau flap (see picture, below right).

These are usually found to be either just over three feet wide or occasionally about two feet wide and I prefer the smaller version which has a single astragal glazed door and can be bought for about £200.

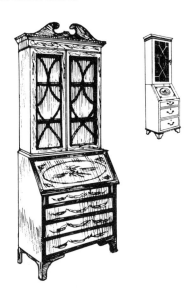

Hepplewhite style bureau bookcase (left) £300

EDWARDIAN BUREAU BOOKCASE

HERE are two bureau bookcases, both dating from about 1900, which illustrate the extraordinarily wide difference between good and bad Edwardian styles.

The domed example, despite its mixture of styles, manages to achieve a certain harmonious charm and, although rather plain when compared

with the inlaid bureau bookcases of the period, is well made and veneered in good quality walnut or mahogany. Similarly well proportioned pieces are to be found with a variety of pediment shapes, and sometimes, ball and claw feet and, although none are likely to win any design awards, they are quite acceptable pieces of furniture by most standards.

Edwardian mahogany bookcase £90
Edwardian oak Bureau bookcase (right) £30

There might be polite words to describe the other piece illustrated but, if there are I don't know them.

There is nothing wrong with a William and Mary style base. There is nothing wrong with Stuart influenced carving. There is nothing wrong with a glass fronted cabinet. But when the three are thrown together by a designer whose asthetic sense is rivalled by that of a retarded dray horse, and when the resultant mess is badly produced by inferior non-craftsmen, it is unlikely that the poorly finished item (ply drawer linings and all) is ever going to receive much in the way of praise or recommendation even though it is better than some of the pieces currently being produced.

CHIPPENDALE SECRETAIRE BOOKCASE

NOT unnaturally, secretaire bookcases were developed at about the same time as bureau bookcases and were dictated by the same fashionable taste.

Chippendale secretaire bookcase £950

This particular example, of mahogany, is clearly built to the design of a master and has all the attributes of our old friend Chippendale. Everything is in harmony, from the proportions of the brass loop handles to the overall, architectural balance of the whole, and even such details as the additional handles on each of the sections (to assist those whose task it was to move and clean behind the piece) are exactly right.

The ogee feet, similar to bracket feet but with a cyma, or double curve, became fashionable from about 1760 and it is details such as this which help enormously in the day to day task of establishing the general date of any piece of furniture.

Early English furniture was usually made of oak, this being the tried and tested native hardwood but, by the end of the 17th century, the more refined tastes of the fashionable town dwellers demanded furniture of more exotic woods such as walnut.

The supply of walnut was met mainly from Europe but, in 1709 an extremely hard winter killed off most of the trees and the French, per-turbed by the depleted state of their stocks, placed an embargo on the export of walnut in 1720.

About 1730, as a result of public pressure, the import duty on Spanish mahogany was lifted and designers were able seriously to turn their attention to exploiting the possibilities of this wood, which is extremely strong and hard.

REGENCY SECRETAIRE BOOKCASE

AS trade was developing and the demand increasing for finer detail, such as astragal glazed doors for example, importers turned their eyes towards Jamaica and the West Indies from where the fine grained Cuban mahogany was obtained and so great was the demand that in 1753 alone, over half a million cubic feet were imported.

This secretaire bookcase, dating from 1820, is more reasonably priced than most at the moment, though it, and pieces like it, seem to be increasing in value from week to week.

It still has the basic shape of an 18th century piece but the classical pediment with its scroll ends is typical of the Regency period as is the delicate carving on the curved pilasters. The centre drawer pulls forward to show multitudinous pigeon holes and drawers within, and the drawer front is lowered by means of brass catches to form an adequate, leather covered writing surface.

Pieces of this kind are made of mahogany or rosewood, the latter being the most expensive, and they always present an attractive and well finished appearance from the outside.

Regency secretaire bookcase £275

A useful, though not absolutely reliable guide to dating a piece such as this is to look closely at the interior fitting of the secretaire drawer; generally speaking, the better the quality the earlier the date. It is often disappointing to find that, among the late 19th century reproductions of earlier furniture, the rule was, "what the eye doesn't see, the heart doesn't grieve" — finely finished exterior surfaces concealing a considerable amount of scrimping on the small drawers and pigeon holes in the fitted compartments of secretaires and bureaux.

A good pair of early 19th century open bookcases in simulated rosewood with painted decoration. £400

VICTORIAN SECRETAIRE BOOKCASE

THIS is one of the most reasonably priced secretaire bookcases to be bought today and is similar to the earlier Victorian bookcases with the addition of a fitted centre drawer between upper and lower sections.

Veneered in mahogany or, occasionally, rather plain walnut, they are to be found in only two qualities—good and not so good—and the earlier examples are generally better than those that followed. They are not particularly beautiful pieces of furniture, admittedly, but they are practical and, in the better quality, fulfil their function very adequately.

A nicely proportioned Georgian breakfront bookcase in mahogany with boxwood string inlay on the panelled cupboard doors. The delicately glazed upper section is surmounted by a dentil cornice; 10 feet wide by 9 feet high.   £1,000

Victorian secretaire bookcase   £90

Some improvement in the appearance of these pieces can be effected by replacing the rather ungainly wooden knobs with pressed brass handles and, although I have seen them doctored up with glazing bars and brass grilles in the panelled doors, I feel this to be wasted effort since, after considerable expenditure of time, effort and money, the article still looks what it is—an acceptable if unexciting Victorian secretaire bookcase.

18th CENTURY BREAKFRONT BOOKCASE

NOW we move on to look at the really big fellows; the breakfront bookcases which were unrivalled for popularity during the 18th century.

These are the largest pieces of furniture to be found and if you are an avid collector of books in the happy position of having a large roomed house and a friendly bank manager, go out at once and buy one, for they are, like the dinosaur, doomed to eventual extinction.

As already mentioned, most earlier bookcases of this type were designed by architects and made to fit a particular wall as the house was built. This being the case, they are either still where they were built or have been demolished along with the houses to which they belonged.

Fortunately for us, furniture designers such as Chippendale, Hepplewhite and the Adams', muscled in on the trade and designed breakfront bookcases in sections in order that they might be moved into and out of houses — though I might add that this requires considerable effort and a large van.

**18th century breakfront bookcase.
£1,100**

While these were all built to the same basic design, with a centre section which protruded from the end pieces, the details of style vary tremendously from the quite plain to the very elaborate and, as such, span a wide range of prices from as little as £250 to upwards of £5,000.

This particular example is a good, average, mahogany breakfront bookcase with astragal glazed doors above and panelled doors below, behind which are shelves.

LATE 18th CENTURY BREAKFRONT SECRETAIRE BOOKCASE

ALTHOUGH that indefatigable commentator on the fashionable taste of his times, Horace Walpole, describes these as "immeasurably ponderous" pieces of furniture, some designs, notably those of Sheraton and Hepplewhite, managed to convey an air of delicacy despite their enormous size (although most are between six and ten feet I have seen them up to 25 feet in width).

The example illustrated is one of the more expensive, 18th century, varieties made of satinwood and beautifully inlaid with urns and ribbons in various coloured woods.

If I have not yet convinced you, these have the added attraction of a secretaire in the centre drawer and a delicately designed cornice.

I have always wanted to own a breakfront bookcase but, unfortunately my taste is rather rich for my pocket and my house has such low ceilings that if I don't bang my head at least three times a day I get an uncomfortable feeling that I am shrinking.

It is worth, however, trying to find an Edwardian reproduction of a piece of this sort for these are considerably less expensive, though, for that reason alone, they are difficult to find since they are nearly always bought as soon as they reach the market.

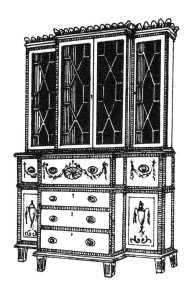

Late 18th century breakfront secretaire bookcase £2,500

19th CENTURY BREAKFRONT BOOKCASE

THIS bookcase with its arched windows and plain glass doors dates from the 19th century and, although not in the same class as the two previous examples, is still a highly desirable piece of furniture.

Most of the 19th century breakfront bookcases are of mahogany, though I have seen some quite extraordinary Victorian examples in oak, big as houses and teeming with carving all over, including near life sized carved animal heads (bears, boars and horses) on the lower doors.

19th century breakfront bookcase £375

As you might expect, expensive pieces like this are commonly reproduced from something less desirable, so look carefully before buying to make sure that you are not giving your money for a converted 19th century wardrobe.

The usual method of making this conversion is to cut the wardrobe in half, giving the lower section a top and reducing the depth of the upper half so that it sits back when replaced. The doors are then remade, those in the lower half with panels and the upper half glazed. Shelves are then fixed into place, and presto, the job is done.

This is one of the few occasions when I think a doctoring job is worthwhile for it creates a highly acceptable piece of furniture out of a big lump which, in these days of fitted wardrobes, is largely obsolete.

Fortunately, none but a very skilled cabinet maker can do the job so well that it is likely to fool any but the most gullible buyer.

Occasional Tables

AFTER many years of careful study and research 1 have calculated that, if all the occasional tables ever made were placed together they would make a heap just three sixteenths of an inch lower than Table Mountain, take longer to paint than the Forth Bridge and the Eiffel Tower put together and provide a surface just large enough to take all the doughnuts consumed in New York in five hundred and twelve years, four months, two weeks, six days, three hours and fifty seven minutes— and I defy anyone to prove me wrong. The shops abound with them and, unless you are impossible to please, there is bound to be something some- where which suits your eye, your decor and your pocket.

The early tables, naturally enough, were made for eating from but, as time passed, there arose a need for specialised tables made to fulfil specific functions. As many of these needs no longer exist, it means that there is now a monumental number of tables of all shapes and sizes in search of a purpose or use.

I have, in the following pages, ignored most of the more usual oc- casional tables which can be bought for under £20—there are so many that it would be impossible to make any kind of logical selection—and have confined myself to those which have some degree of interest beyond the usual function of a table.

WILLIAM & MARY SIDE TABLE

SIDE tables are the root from which occasional tables grew, dating from the 15th century and resembling in their earliest form, a kind of chest of drawers under a table top. They were used in large households only, for storage of cutlery, linen and condiments in the dining room and, true to the fashion of the time, were made of oak. Few of these have survived and as such command exceptionally high prices.

There are quite a few to be found, however, dating from the William and Mary period, which although expensive, are a good investment.

The example illustrated is of walnut, superbly inlaid with arabesque mar- quetry, and it dates from about 1690 as is indicated by the nicely turned legs, cross stretchers and bun feet. Slightly better side tables from this period have shaped stretchers with S scroll legs ending in volutes while others, even more exotic, can be found to have tops overlaid with chased and embossed silver and matching mirrors, also of silver.

LOWBOY

LOWBOYS were popular through- out the 18th century and fell into two main types—the town-made and country-made pieces. The town-made lowboys were inclined to be more so- phisticated in style and materials, usually of mahogany or walnut with cabriole legs, while those of the country made variety, usually of oak or elm, tended to be rather plainer and more functional looking.

Their chief attraction lying in their versatility, lowboys may be used as just another table in the room, as a writing table or, with a mirror, as a dressing table.

I have an affection for lowboys which dates back to the first day of my antique dealing career—the day after I left school.

Leaving home bright and early with ten painstakingly saved pounds in my pocket, not knowing quite what an

William and Mary side table £400

George I walnut lowboy (top) £300
18th century oak lowboy (below)£160

65

antique was or where I was going to find any, I set out determined to begin a career as an antique dealer.

The handwritten postcard in the news-agent's window read something like ". . . Must sell. Writing table £1." I popped around to the address given and there it was. It looked old so I paid up and staggered with it to the nearest antique shop.

Feeling both frightened and cheeky, I demanded, in as mature a manner as I could manage, a fiver for my writing table and was very surprised indeed when the dealer paid up with a smile. To encourage a young newcomer to the business he said.

Thinking back, I cannot remember ever having bought or sold a better lowboy—and the dealer I sold that one to swears to this day that he only sold it for seven!

VICTORIAN SIDE TABLE

THIS nice little Victorian side table dates from about 1850 and can be bought very cheaply today.

Soon after this one was made, the fine tapering legs gave way to massive turned ones with heavy brass cup castors and the whole look of the thing became bulbous and rather ugly.

Usually, these are made of solid mahogany with a fine grain which takes a deep, true polish but I have seen them in pine and these, stripped and waxed, will be found suitable for any room in the house.

Victorian papier mache occasional table decorated with a hand painted floral spray.

Victorian side table £25

A nineteenth century, amboyna wood library table inlaid with ebony.

Tables of this type are attributed to the architect William Butterfield who favoured them in satin walnut with ebony inlay, though many had white marble tops and these are ideal for serving drinks.

EAGLE CONSOLE TABLE

CONSOLE tables are so named for the console, or bracket, which is used to support them against the wall in the absence of back legs.

Perhaps surprisingly, their development came later than that of most other tables for they did not appear until the early 18th century, when house interiors became more sophisticated, with furniture being designed to blend into the entire decorative scheme. It was not, in fact, until about 1730 that these eagle console tables achieved real popularity following their appearance in the court of Louis XIV where, as a rule, they were placed beneath a pier glass and sported superbly figured tops of Italian marble.

Eagle console table £575

Owing to their rather flamboyant nature, tables of this kind were always well made, their beautifully carved pine eagles with outstretched wings grasping a tortoise in one claw, usually on a rocky base. The eagle would normally have been gilded and the base given a marbled effect.

Originally, they were made in pairs, but alas, time has separated most of them. On the rare occasions that a pair do go up for sale, the price usually soars to three or four times that which a single will fetch.

VICTORIAN CONSOLE TABLE

THIS more conveniently styled console table with its fine rococo ornamentation and shaped top was originally introduced during the 18th

Victorian console table (left) £150 Small 18th century console table (right) £250

century but, fortunately, it was extensively copied during the Victorian rococo revival and some of these copies are still available today.

Although not as expensive as the 18th century originals, the Victorian reproductions are not cheap, partly as a result of their poor survival record;

the heavy marble slab tops proving too much for many relatively frail frames which were produced to support them. On the original tables, the marble tops were regarded as being by far the most important features (console tables were described as "marble slab frames" in early inventories) and they were carefully selected for fine grain and exquisite colour gradation. and harmony from such notable suppliers as Signor Domenico de Angualis. The Victorians having rather less flamboyant tastes, tended to go more for plain white tops in preference to the pinks and greens of the earlier examples and were inclined to build up the rococo ornamentation with gesso instead of producing the fine, gilded carving of the original period.

LATE VICTORIAN CONSOLE TABLE

THIS cross between a console table and a washstand might, at first glance, be regarded as ugly. On its own, it is ugly but, strangely, I have seen it (or one just like it) slotted quite majestically into a roomful of other Victorian furniture.

Generally made of either walnut or mahogany, the frame is normally about three feet six inches wide, though it has a younger brother about two feet

A superb, eighteenth century, Italian, carved gilt wood console table decorated with female figures and putti.

wide with a single cabriole leg support which will fit quite nicely into the average hallway.

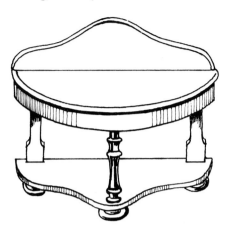

Late Victorian console table £15

At the risk of causing considerable distress to purists and traditionalists, all of whom are hereby warned that they may find the following paragraphs offensive, I have a suggestion for those who might like to make their own console tables from another, cheaper piece of Victorian furniture.

There are any number of small, six legged Victorian tables about which were designed to stand in the centre of a room but which are now, alas, unfashionable and unwanted.

By the simple expedient of sawing one of these in half lengthwise, two delightful little console tables may be made, each with three legs, which simply need fixing to the wall on either side of a window or doorway.

A delightful little Indian occasional table intricately decorated with ivory, circa 1870. £65

BUTLER'S TRAY

SHERATON, never at a loss for a zippy description, called this "a Sideboard for the Butler, who has the Care of the Liquor at a Gentleman's Table" and trays such as these were designed to be placed on an X-shaped folding stand of turned or, later, in the Regency varieties, square sectioned wood.

Butler's tray £100

The butler's tray illustrated is one of the commoner varieties, having an oval shape with brass-hinged flaps which fold upward to form a rectangular tray carried by means of the shaped holes in opposite flaps.

Naturally, a hard, dark wood was most practical for the construction of a tray of this kind, likely to have various drinks spilled upon it, and Spanish mahogany was the timber most widely employed as being hard enough to be impervious to most liquors and dark enough not to show the stains of those to which it is not.

Butler's trays are reproduced in vast quantities today (doubtless because of the high prices fetched by originals) and, as they are often made from old timber, reproductions can be extremely difficult for a professional buyer to detect and virtually impossible for an amateur.

All I can suggest in this respect is that you ask the vendor for a receipt which clearly states the supposed age of the tray for, under the terms of the Trade Descriptions Act, you will be able to obtain redress if you later find that you have bought a modern reproduction in the belief that it was an old, original piece.

PARQUETRY TOP TABLE

Regency parquetry top table £145

THIS particularly fine quality occasional table from the Regency period is made of rosewood with beautifully delicate carving on the three supports round the centre of the column.

The top is of parquetry (which is a mosaic of variously coloured geometrically shaped pieces of wood mounted on a softwood base, as opposed to marquetry, an inlay work of pictorial designs), an early form of decoration found in France and Italy some time before it made its way to Britain during the William and Mary period.

Parquetry tops, unfortunately, are rather difficult to live with and need to be treated with some care if they are not to spoil.

The two things they particularly don't like are damp and heat—water left on the surface or the table placed too near the central heating will cause the little sections of wood to curl up like last week's British Rail sandwiches.

INVALID TABLE

ALTHOUGH this is called an invalid table, there are so many around that their use cannot have been confined solely to the Victorian sick. Even without the wonder drugs of the 20th century, no society can possibly have been that sick and survived.

Designed so that the lower half could be pushed out of the way under the bed with the table top extending across the invalid's mid section in a suitable position to allow meals to be taken, letters to be written, wills signed and jig saw puzzles assembled on its surface, the invalid table was so practical an innovation that it is still produced today. Modern invalid tables, however, are made from tubular steel and plastic laminates, these materials being considered more hygenic, if less attractive, than their mahogany or walnut forebears.

Invalid table £16

Besides being ideal for breakfast in bed (always assuming a partner prepared to get up and do the work), invalid tables can be used almost anywhere in the house as an extra surface by the side of table or chair. This is made more convenient by virtue of the fact that most invalid tables are adjustable for height by means of a fitment in the stem.

VICTORIAN GIPSY TABLE

HERE is a handy (get it, handy—palm—fortune telling—gipsy) little table which was popular in the later stages of the Victorian period.

It has three bobbin-turned legs, usually of beech though occasionally of rosewood, which cross in the centre below the velvet covered top with its fringe all round.

Victorian gipsy table £8

These are the tables at which Romany fortune tellers traditionally sit when laying out the Tarot pack, crystal gazing or simply reading palms and the basic design is one which would have developed quite naturally among a wandering people lacking workshop facilities.

Gipsies have not always travelled around in caravans, the vardo only having been seen since the beginning of the 19th century. Prior to that time (and, to a lesser extent, since) gipsies travelled on foot or horseback with very few artifacts, relying for their living on their wits and their skill at improvising everything from tent poles to tables.

The gipsy table is simply an extension of the tripod which, as a stable support, has been known to man for thousands of years and which, by virtue of the fact that it can be made perfectly adequately out of three poles

and a length of string, formed the basis of most gipsy constructions (including their earliest tents). It is not surprising, therefore, to find that an enterprising cabinet maker, recognising the simplicity and practicability of this table design should have manufactured them and, naturally, when gipsies began owning more possessions and carrying them in mobile houses, they preferred the familiar style.

TUNBRIDGE WARE TABLE

FOLLOWING the discovery of mineral springs at Tunbridge Wells by Lord North in the early part of the 17th century, a tourist industry grew and, of the many objects produced to meet the demand for souvenirs, articles inlaid with woods of various colours proved most popular.

Earliest forms of Tunbridge ware were of geometric patterns, similar to parquetry, but this quickly developed into representations of landscapes, buildings and scenic views, generally contained within fine borders. Unlike parquetry, however, Tunbridge ware was made from thin strips of wood glued together and then fret-cut into the thin layers which were veneered on to a variety of objects from small boxes to table tops.

**19th century
Tunbridge ware table £135**

Despite the foul taste of the water drawn from Tunbridge Wells, enough people visited the town and bought objects of Tunbridge ware, for the craft survived throughout the 19th century.

On large surfaces, a cube pattern proved very popular, the various visible surfaces of the cubes being suggested by clever selection of natural woods—dyeing of wood being considered infra dig.

BLACKAMOOR TABLE

Blackamoor table £175

AN absolute necessity in fashionable 18th century households was a blackamoor figure and this could be either standing alone, or incorporated into the design of a table, candelabra or torchere.

With an insularity that has changed but little in two centuries, our 18th century forebears lumped everyone with negro characteristics into a single category — blackamoor — in the fond belief that everyone who looked like that was Moorish, and blackamoor figures were realistically carved in pine before being painted in a highly coloured representation of an oriental livery, again on the assumption that "they all dress like that out there . . ."

The slave traders began the whole thing in the first place by importing negro children for use as servants in fashionable houses. But demand outstripped supply and the children, with characteristic disregard for their masters, grew up, so people began to make do with carved figures instead. Distasteful as all this is, it has left a legacy of beautiful figures which fully deserve the considerable sums they fetch at auction.

It was claimed that blackamoor figures, when placed discreetly near windows, served as anti-burglar devices, though it is a little hard to believe that even an 18th century villain would be fooled and I would hesitate to recommend this as a valuable function of these figures.

There was a resurgence of popularity between 1850 and 1870, during which period little girls were produced as well as little boys—the reason for this was perfectly respectable and has to do with the efforts of Mr. Wilberforce in abolishing the slave trade.

DUMB-WAITER

DUMB-WAITERS were extremely fashionable during the final quarter of the 18th century and throughout the Regency period, although there is evidence that they were available as early as 1727, when Lord Bristol purchased one from a cabinet maker named Robert Leigh.

It was Sheraton, with a turn of phrase as elegant as one of his own chairlegs, who described the dumb-waiter as "a useful piece of furniture to serve in some respects the place of a waiter, whence it is so named".

Dumb-waiter (left) £185
18th century dumb-waiter (right) £160

Generally consisting of three or four graduated shelves revolving around a central column, dumb-waiters were usually made with tripod bases termin-

ating in feet whose style varied with the transient fashions of the period. The shelves, largest at the bottom, were sometimes made from single pieces of wood and sometimes constructed with hinged flaps (as illustrated).

Dumb-waiters were made to be placed at the corners of the dining table where guests could help themselves and, as Miss Mary Hamilton commented somewhat provocatively ". . . conversation was not under any restraint by ye servants being in ye room."

I wonder what they talked about?

MOORISH TABLE

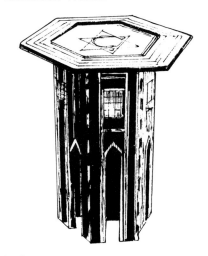

19th century Moorish table £7.50

THE Victorian mania for oriental furniture was reflected in the advertising of a number of large stores who boasted of having an entire floor devoted to the stuff, ranging from elephants' feet through lacquered bamboo and Indian brass tables to this Moorish table.

Tables of this kind are usually quite small and consist of a six to twelve sided, collapsible framework which supports a table top whose shape is dictated by the number of legs on the base. Their most notable feature is the inlay work of bone, ivory, shell, various metals and different coloured woods, many table tops sporting all these and just about everything else the craftsman could think of to stick on.

Generally of rather poor workmanship, these tables are fairly widespread but, just occasionally, an exquisite example turns up.

Inveterate sale-goers may have seen, from time to time, vaguely Georgian looking furniture of about the right age but rather poorly made of a number of strange woods. This is usually to be found at the sale of effects of an ex-colonial chap who, homesick for England, has thrust a more or less accurate pencil sketch under the nose of an eastern cabinet maker with instructions to "make one of these . . ." The poor fellow, never having seen the actual style, would have done his best but the handicap was usually too great.

The tendency for this and the traditionally styled eastern furniture to fall apart is not altogether a result of poor workmanship: once our ex-colonial has returned to Cheltenham and set up home, and the English climate has had a few years to get to work on his precious furniture, warping begins, joints open and the craftsman is blamed.

TRICOTEUSE

IF you see one of these (and there are not many to be seen in antique shops) and it is reasonably priced, buy it!

In design, the tricoteuse owes much to late 18th century Sheraton influence, though most, if not all, on the market today date from the late 19th century revival of these styles. Generally of mahogany with boxwood string inlay on the shelves, an occasional piece may be found of satinwood, inlaid with delicate flower and ribbon motifs.

19th century tricoteuse £240

Tricoteuses (if that's how you spell it), were designed to stand in the centres of rooms, among the guests, with goodies displayed on the undershelf and the tea things on the upper tray,

which could be lifted off by means of brass handles.

Really beautifully made, these are a credit to the craftsmen of the late 19th century and are delightfully feminine without being fussy.

18th CENTURY TEA TABLE

THE universal elixir — excellent for failing eyesight and a certain cure for the defluxions (and you can look that one up for yourself)—that was the accepted value of tea when it was introduced in the mid 17th century.

The serving of this superior beverage provided the impetus for a spate of gadgetry including teapoys, kettle-stands and, of course, small tea tables which were placed beside chairs for individual use.

The small table illustrated dates from the mid 18th century and is not to be confused with the little reproduction wine tables which may be bought today for about £15. It stands about two feet high, has a spindle gallery and a tip-up top in order that it will stand close against the wall when not in use.

18th century tea table £85

Tables of this kind became extremely popular from about 1750 when tea began to be taken in the home more than in tea shops, which were beginning to earn a reputation for licentiousness on the part of their habituees.

This nicely proportioned, English mahogany reading table, supported on a carved tripod base, has an unusual adjustable top and a single drawer.

71

ARCHITECT'S TABLE

THE late 18th century saw a sudden surge of interest in architecture on an amateur level—every gentleman of fashion was fairly bursting with buildings which just had to be planned, if not actually built, and the great need was for a table of a size and shape to serve the needs of the enthusiastic aesthete.

This table is typical of the furniture makers' attempts to supply the demand and is made of mahogany with squared legs, the front pair halving to allow a full length drawer to be supported when it is pulled forward.

The interior of the drawer usually contains a slide to provide extra surface area and, beneath this, small drawers and partitions are provided for storing pens, brushes and so on.

Architect's table   £265

The table top on the piece illustrated is adjustable by means of ratchets underneath, while others have a double top which can be raised in order to give the user a choice of either standing or sitting while he works. Still others have a pop-up ledge which springs up when the top is raised and serves to support a book or to stop pens from rolling on to the floor.

GUERIDON TABLE

IN the mid 17th century, small candlestands, often in the shape of a negro holding a platform, were introduced to enable lighting to be more conveniently placed in the room. Being of negro form, they were often referred to as gueridons, which was the name given to the young negro brought from Africa to act as servants in the larger, more wealthy households.

19th century gueridon table £150

As is so often the case, the passage of time and common usage caused the name no longer to relate solely to its proper object, gueridon being accepted as applicable to any small table designed to support candles or a lamp. By the end of the century, there were any number of styles in common use, particularly carved and gilded designs which came from France, from where most of today's surviving pieces come.

This pleasant little gueridon table is from the Louis Philippe period (1830-1848) when French styles were particularly decorative. It is veneered in kingwood, which is not unlike rosewood, has ormolu mounts and a fine ormolu gallery surrounding the rose pink marble top, with a drawer below.

Being small, these tables can be placed anywhere in the house but are particularly suited to use as bedside tables supporting lamps—the original purpose for which they were designed.

SPECIMEN TABLE

THE squirrel instinct has always been fairly strong, as has the desire to show off the collections of hoarded things in the best manner possible. Nineteenth century recognition of this fact caused a spate of specially designed cabinets and tables

EARLY GEORGIAN ROOM

The reign of George I might well be described as the first golden age of English furniture design.

The introduction of mahogany, with its fine grained strength and rich colour, allowed cabinet-makers an entirely new freedom in the pursuit of elegance and style as can be seen in the superb lines of the cabriole-leg chair with its flowing arm supports and richly carved centre splat.

The small gallery table, set for tea, stands on a finely carved tripod base. The walnut bureau has a nicely fitted interior and dates from about 1730.

(Courtesy Geffrye Museum)

made particularly for the purpose of displaying small objects from fossils to fans and the specimen tables illustrated are good examples.

Specimen tables usually fall into one of three categories: good, not so good and early exotic, and all are more expensive than they ought to be since they appeal to one of the most fundamental traits in human nature—pride of possession. The two most often seen are made of mahogany, earlier examples having boxwood string inlay and straight tapered legs, while later tables were plain with shaped legs and an undershelf.

Mahogany with boxwood inlay (centre) £65
Plain mahogany (left) £45
Heart shaped (right) £165

Best examples and, therefore, most expensive, have heart shaped tops with floral marquetry or have fine ormolu mounts and are made of exotic woods such as kingwood. Although the interior fabric may have become worn this may be easily replaced with a fine velvet, without detracting from the value.

Most people prefer to have their collections of treasures and valuables on display rather than tucked away in a safe and, with the variety of anti-theft devices on the market, the risk involved in doing this can be minimal—each police district has its Crime Prevention Officer who can advise on suitable methods of safeguarding your property.

QUARTETTE TABLE

QUARTETTE tables became popular during the latter half of the 18th century and have remained so ever since.

Price and quality vary considerably but all quartette tables conform to the same general specifications; three or four small, graduated tables which slide away, each beneath the next largest, and which always tend to be unstable in use.

They have slender legs with single stretchers which act as supports and serve as stops to prevent the tables sliding about when they are put together.

Earlier quartettes (or nests of tables as they are sometimes called) were usually made of plain mahogany while the Regency styles tended more towards flamboyance, often being made of rosewood with brass string inlays. The Victorian period saw a wide assortment of styles and shapes from square to oval, made in a variety of woods and finishes, including ornately lacquered decoration.

The two nasty things about these tables are their inability (as I have already mentioned) to stand firm and do the job they were made for and their extraordinarily high price.

Not much can be done about the prices, I fear, but, if you feel you can never be happy unless you own a quartette of tables, I would suggest

Quartette table: Regency (left) £375
George III (top right) £175
Edwardia (below right) £40

you choose very carefully, with an eye to stability, settling for a reproduction set if necessary, since these tend to have stronger legs and are more serviceable.

STRETCHER TABLE

THE 19th century must have abounded with small stretcher tables, in a variety of woods, which are reasonably priced (usually under £45) and reasonably well made.

An average size would be about three feet long by 15 inches wide, though there are a good number about which are some four feet six inches long and these, because they will serve admirably as dining tables, tend to be somewhat more expensive.

Stretcher table:
Victorian beech (top left) £22.50
Early Victorian (top right) £35
Victorian Walnut (below) £45

The three examples illustrated are those most commonly found in shops; and reading, as the best captions always do, from left to right, they are a late Victorian piece of polished beech, a burr walnut veneered table with barley twist supports and boxwood string inlay dating from about 1850 and an earlier Victorian example of plain mahogany which retains a hint of Regency influence.

Being narrow these tend to be slightly awkward for use as tea tables but, against a wall in the hall or lounge they are ideal for displaying bric a brac or a bowl of flowers.

Chests

A chest of drawers, as the name implies, is simply a chest which has been equipped with a series of drawers in order that all items placed within it are (or should be) reasonably accessible.

The practice of setting drawers in the base of a lidded coffer originated on the Continent in the middle of the 16th century and British furniture makers were quick then, as now, to take advantage of stylish innovations from across the Channel.

Little progress was made for the following 100 years, and the dull, heavy garments approved by the Puritan age did not suffer unduly from being folded and laid in chests with, maybe, blankets or other heavy clothes on top of them. As time progressed, however, and the British taste in clothes began to lean once again towards delicacy and ornament, relatively shallow drawers were found to provide compact storage without crushing and creasing the finer fabrics under masses of other linen.

By this time, the standard article would have had a number of drawers in the lower section with cupboard doors above and, often, a hinged lid enclosing a small well above these.

This design was relatively short lived. By the end of the reign of Charles II (1660–1685) the chest of drawers as we know it today had emerged and, although there have been minor stylistic variations, the endurance of the basic design is proof enough that the chest of drawers had gone about as far as it could go up the evolutionary ladder.

NONE of us is likely to stumble on a chest like this but I feel that it is worth including here if only to illustrate the early development of the chest of drawers. Having said that, and knowing the capriciousness of the of the antique game, I fully expect every antique shop in every high street throughout the country to suddenly produce at least one of them within the next few days, all at give-away prices . . . . .

Since the article was a Continental innovation, it is not unnatural that the decoration should reflect the tastes of France, Germany and Holland. Generally, this took the form of geometrical panels, often inlaid with bone, ivory, ebony and, occasionally, mother of pearl.

CHARLES II CHEST 1670

Charles II chest, 1670 £475

Throughout the transitional period from coffer to chest of drawers, there were a great many variations on the basic theme but, eventually, a practical and attractive formula emerged (about 1670). This piece, with its lidded top enclosing a well above cupboard doors, dates from that period.

It is surprising how furniture of this period was often beautifully decorated (usually by imported craftsmen) until it is remembered that it reflects the exuberance of people freed at last from the plain, puritanical Cromwellian regime during which anything ostentatious or elaborately decorative was considered offensive and likely to prove a kind of lightning tree for outbursts of divine wrath.

CHARLES II CHEST OF DRAWERS 1680

Charles II chest of drawers, £260

NO sooner were the Puritans out of the way than the British began to need more drawers (!) in which to store their fine clothes and all the other odds and ends of frippery which were associated at that time with gracious living. Not slow to respond to the demand, cabinet makers produced vast quantities of chests of drawers, employing, as a rule, the familiar native wood, oak, for the purpose.

The architectural geometric mouldings proved popular as decoration and these were glued and bradded in position—a practice which continues to to the present day.

This example, dating from about 1680, appears to have eight drawers but has, in fact, only four long ones —the central panel being raised to give a fashionable impression of more drawers than there actually were.

If you think you have seen one of these knocking about in your local junk shop for a fiver—you haven't. Reproductions were produced in great quantities during the Jacobean revival at the end of the Victorian era.

Just in case, though, take out a drawer and see the provision that was made for it to slide in and out; if the drawer has deep slots in the sides, which slide on runners fixed to the carcase of the piece, you may just be in luck . . . . .

WILLIAM AND MARY WALNUT CHEST

AS taste developed, there arose a need for more sophisticated chests in more exotic woods such as this walnut veneer which was put on to an oak or pine carcase.

The use of veneers made the manufacture of moulded drawer fronts impractical and, consequently, more emphasis was placed on the figuring of the veneers as a decorative feature. The oyster design on this example results from careful cutting of the veneer from a tree bough. This is glued vertically on to the drawer front, the figuring being meticulously matched, and it is crossbanded on the edges, often with an intermediate herringbone inlay.

The drawers are now found to slide on the horizontal partitions which separate them and they are finely dovetailed, where earlier they were more crudely jointed or even nailed together.

It is, unfortunately, quite common to find cracks in the tops and sides of furniture of this period resulting from the practice of constructing the carcases of one inch thick planks of oak or pine which were simply glued together along their edges.

This has proved unsatisfactory, for there was no provision for the different rates of expansion and contraction of the carcases and their veneers and there is little that can be done to restore such pieces to an unblemished condition.

William and Mary walnut chest £350

EARLY 18th CENTURY BACHELOR CHEST

Early 18th century bachelor chest £1,400

BEFORE I start enthusing about the superb workmanship and beautiful proportions of this delicious piece of furniture, glance quickly at the sort of price it is likely to demand and decide whether it is worth reading on . . . . .

Yes? Of course, the single criterion against which the monetary value of any antique article must be judged is "What can you get for it?" Believe me, this piece is worth the money but you have to be either very flush or very bold to buy it.

It stands between 2ft. 9in. and 3ft. 9in. high on its bracket feet and is between 2ft. and 2ft. 9in. wide. The folding top, which was designed for brushing clothes upon but serves equally well as a writing surface, is supported on pull out supports placed on either side of the top drawer.

These bachelor chests have four drawers, veneered in burr walnut, with, as a rule, plain walnut on the sides of the pine or oak carcases.

Although they continued to be made throughout the 18th century, these were usually of mahogany and it is the earlier, walnut veneered, pieces which really fetch the money.

Mouldings between the drawers were half round prior to 1715. From then until about 1725, two half rounds were placed side by side and then, after 1725, cockbeading was employed to provide a small lip on the edges of the drawers.

MID 18th CENTURY
CHEST OF DRAWERS

**Mid 18th century
chest of drawers £215**

WALNUT continued as the most favoured wood for chests of drawers until the middle of the 18th century, when it gave way to Spanish mahogany.

Usually of rectangular form with two short and three long drawers, chests were generally straight fronted and quite plain during this period, though a few of the really fine quality pieces had canted corners or delicate Chinese lattice work decoration.

An early eighteenth century walnut bachelor chest with a folding top and bracket feet.

Handles can be a useful pointer to the age of a piece of furniture, though not, I hasten to add, infallible, for they were continually swapped around or replaced.

Earliest handles were brass drop loops which were held on to the back-plates with brass or iron wire or, after 1700 by the heads of nutted bolts.

Pierced backplates date from about 1720 and continued to be used, with the addition of ornamental key escutcheons, until about 1750, when sunken escutcheons began to be used. The heavier brass loop handles began to be used in 1735, and each bolt head is mounted on a separate backplate.

LATE 18th CENTURY
BOWFRONTED CHEST,

ALTHOUGH some bowfronted chests were produced at about the same time as the straightfronted ones, they failed to achieve popularity until near the end of the 18th century and may not have succeeded even then had they not found a staunch advocate in the person of Hepplewhite.

He revelled in bow and serpentine fronts, convinced that these flowing shapes displayed the virtues of the canted corners to still further advantage.

**Late 18th century
Bowfronted chest £215**

Here, the feet, slightly splayed, reflect a French influence, and the line is enhanced by the use of a nicely shaped apron.

Once again, attention should be centred on the oak lined drawers as a guide to date of manufacture, for it was in about 1770 that a constructional change occurred.

Until this time, the drawer bottoms were made with the grain of the wood running front to back but, from this time onward, the grain will be found to run from side to side, the bottom often being made of two separate pieces of wood supported by a central bearer.

GEORGE III CHEST WITH SLIDE

THERE were any number of straightfronted, mahogany chests of drawers produced in the final years of the 18th century, but the feature which lifts this example from the mass is the return of the brushing slide, set above the top drawer, which had not been a feature of chests since Queen Anne departed this life.

This slide was designed to ensure that there would always be a clear surface available on which clothes could be laid while being brushed, though it is probable that it was also conceived of as a useful and comfortable writing surface which, by virtue of the fact that it is retractable, obviated the waste of space which would have been occasioned by the provision of a kneehole.

The oak, or mahogany, framed slide pulls out like a drawer with two brass knobs or minute drop loop handles.

Early carcases are of solid mahogany with oak lined drawers and, as a rule, are on bracket feet.

The general rule for all furniture these days is: the smaller the better, and prices increase inversely with the size of the article. Thus, chests under about two feet six inches wide are likely to command as much as twice the price of their larger, more common, fellows.

George III chest with slide (3ft. wide) £225

EARLY 19th CENTURY COROMANDEL WOOD CHEST

MOST late 18th century chests have pine carcases veneered with mahogany and fitted with oak drawer linings. The mahogany was often enlivened by means of lines of ebony or satinwood and with fine inlaid conch shells set in oval frames.

As the Regency period developed its more flamboyant use of decoration,

Early 19th century coromandel wood chest £325

Typical Victorian chest of drawers, veneered in walnut, with turned wooden handles.

chests veneered in boldly figured foreign woods became popular, particularly those in rosewood or, as illustrated, in coromandel.

Coromandel wood has a very distinctive dark brown and yellow figuring (like an exaggerated rosewood) and is a member of the ebony family which grows on the Coromandel coast in south east India.

It is a superbly hard wood which polishes to a magnificent shine and is seen at its most attractive when used on some of the vanity boxes and writing slopes made in the early 19th century, many of which are delightfully enhanced with brass inlay.

VICTORIAN BOWFRONT CHEST OF DRAWERS

THERE could never be any doubt that this ponderously heavy, bow-fronted chest of drawers dates from the Victorian period.

It is veneered in beautifully figured mahogany, has a lip on the top edge and stands upon good, fat bun feet. Note, too, the usual Victorian knobs on the drawers—these were introduced, according to the manufacturers, to save cleaning, though I suspect that economy in the manufacturing stage had rather more to do with it.

I have seen these pieces improved by the removal of the bottom drawer (and surrounding portion of carcase) and the addition of bracket feet. This tends to reduce somewhat the ponderous appearance and the effect can be carried further by replacing the knobs with brass handles and grooving the lip (if you will pardon the expression!).

Look carefully before buying what purports to be a more desirable 18th century chest—it may be one of these tarted up in the manner described.

Victorian bowfront chest of drawers £45

VICTORIAN STRIPPED PINE CHEST OF DRAWERS

AS a rule, these have two short and two long drawers with turned wooden knobs and short bun feet and, whether rough or already stripped, they are among the best buys on the market today.

They can be bought almost anywhere, hidden under almost their own weight of paint for between £1 and £8, cheaper ones being over 3ft wide.

For those prepared to rush in where angels fear to tread, this is how to strip pine.

Victorian pine chest of drawers, stripped   £20

First, if the article is painted, try Nitromors water washable paint remover: applying it to a small section at a time, removing the resulting goo with a scraper and then medium grade wire wool.   Remove any red stains with Vim, give the whole piece a good scrub down and, when it is thoroughly dry, sand and wax polish.

More stubborn articles need caustic soda but, be warned, this is a vicious and extremely dangerous substance whose use requires the utmost care, and *all* of the following: a large concrete floor; running cold water; vinegar; a nylon brush; rubber boots and gloves and a polythene bucket.

Pour a kettle full of water into the bucket and then, AT ARM'S LENGTH, add a small amount of caustic soda (¼lb. per quart).   Never pour the water on to the dry caustic soda as this can cause a minor explosion.

Having well primed the article to be stripped with cold water first, brush your caustic solution carefully on to the old paint or varnish until it peels off.   Wash the article thoroughly with running water and neutralise with vinegar (it contains acetic acid, a weak solution of which will do as well). Allow to dry then sand and wax as before.

Having explained how to do it, I can only now advise you to ignore the foregoing and pay a professional a tenner to do the job for you. Please remember—caustic soda is a dangerous substance which can cause dreadful burns on unprotected skin and blindness if it is allowed to come into contact with the eyes.

LATE VICTORIAN MAHOGANY CHEST OF DRAWERS

IF you have one of these to sell and call in a dealer, his reaction will be "Oh yes. Very nice. But, sorry, I haven't got room for it in my shop at the moment."   And no wonder, for although this is a beautifully made piece and finely veneered, it really is a great lump of Victorian dross—all barley twist pillars and bun feet, with a shaped top drawer to boot!

Late Victorian mahogany chest of drawers   £12

Having so lightly dismissed this monumental piece of Victorian workmanship, I am reminded that all the seers were equally dismissive about the Victorian cabriole leg chairs a few years ago.   That is how it is with furniture; one minute a dealer will consider himself insulted if he is offered a particular piece and the next, he is chasing all over the country flashing pound notes in search of a ditto, as the catalogue say.

So, you there, quietly storing away all the late Victorian mahogany chests of drawers that you can lay your hands on, waiting for fashions to change: Good on yer!

An early nineteenth century teak military chest with sunken brass handles

EDWARDIAN CHEST
OF DRAWERS

Edwardian chest of drawers £8

HERE is one ugly duckling that definitely does not stand a snowflake's chance of turning into a swan. Ever.

At least the Victorian job had quality of construction working for it, but this one is just plain bad.

You could have bought this at the turn of the century in a choice of solid walnut, mahogany or ash for about £12 and you would have had a 3ft. 6in. wardrobe with a bevelled glass door, a 3ft. dressing chest and mirror, a 3ft. washstand with cupboard and towel rail and a pair of bedroom chairs, all in the same grisly style, thrown in for good measure!

It never ceases to amaze me that an age as elegant as the Edwardian should have found itself lumbered with junk like this when something approaching the Regency would not have gone amiss. The choice of heavy lumps is all the more baffling considering the wealth of Art Nouveau designs which were circulating at this time.

WILLIAM AND MARY CHEST
ON STAND

TOWARDS the end of the 17th century, many chests were raised on stands; often with an extra drawer in the lower section. The reason for this may have been to create a sense of fit proportion between furniture and the high ceilinged rooms of the period, or it may have reflected the stiff backed deportment which was considered proper at that time, raising furniture to a height at which the operative parts could be reached without stooping or bending in an unfashionable manner.

Legs of stands were either turned or, as illustrated, barley twist, and were braced with shaped stretchers and ended in bun feet.

There were a few pieces made of oak but most, if we are to judge by the survivors, were made of pine with walnut veneer and oak lined drawers. Some sport fine arabesque marquetry decoration, their tops having an oval design in the centre and triangular corner pieces. There are half round mouldings between drawers which, with the ovolo lip on the top of the stand, are characteristic of pieces of this period.

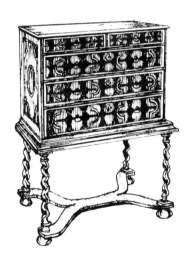

William and Mary chest on stand £500

It is not uncommon to find later bases under these pieces for, although they were generally pretty well made, when full they were inclined to be just that bit too heavy for the rather delicate stands on which they originally stood. This, of course, affects the prices tremendously, those with replaced bases fetching from half to two thirds the price of totally original articles.

LATE GEORGIAN ROOM

As the eighteenth century progressed, furniture became increasingly delicate and feminine as designers pursued the whims of fashion.

The late Georgian room pictured opposite contains furniture representing the height of late eighteenth century elegance: the slender-framed Hepplewhite shield back chair stands beside an interesting tea-table whose two back legs swivel out to support the folding top when open. The Windsor chair has an unusual fret cut centre splat and a saddle seat of nicely figured elm.

(Courtesy Geffrye Museum)

GEORGE I CHEST ON STAND

ALTHOUGH of delicate constitution, the chest on a stand continued to be made in the early part of the 18th century but, instead of the barley twist legs with shaped stretchers, we find that the later pieces have flowing cabriole legs with ball and claw feet and acanthus leaf decoration on the knees.

The stand has one long, and two short drawers and the top is equipped with fluted columns headed by Corinthian capitals, the cornice protruding to accommodate them.

George I chest on stand   £700

Marquetry decoration being out of favour at this time, great use was made of the figuring of burr walnut as a decorative feature, particularly on the drawer fronts. Here the quartering was beautifully executed to give those so nearly symmetrical designs which seem to delight children, resembling, as they do, the designs created by folding a piece of paper on which is a wet ink or paint blob.

When buying one of these, clamber atop a nearby chair and have a look at the top surface of the chest. If you come across one that has been polished, it probably began its life as an ordinary chest of drawers which was adapted by an eager dealer with an eye to quick profits. Since the tops of these chests are above the eye level of all but your friendly neighbourhood

giant, they were normally left unveneered and, unless there is a particularly good explanation for a polished top, you can expect to part with far less money than would be asked for an original piece.

VICTORIAN CHEST ON A STAND

THE chest on a stand, having once been ousted by the more widely accepted chest of drawers, just gave up the fight and did not appear on the scene again until some anonymous Victorian designer, probably claiming the innovation as his own, slipped the style in among all the other reproductions of earlier furniture that were produced during the 19th century.

As so often happened in cases of this sort, however, the man who tried to update the piece completely missed the point and, instead of producing an improved version of the chest on a stand, came up with this sadly deformed construction. Bracket feet might have suited it quite well, and higher cabriole legs could have done the trick but no; instead, we have something which looks as though it has been chopped off at the knees.

Victorian chest on a stand   £50

As a rule, these chests are veneered in mahogany or rather plain walnut with brass loop handles and brass key escutcheons.

Although not well favoured as regards design, this is a fairly practical piece of furniture with easy to get at

top drawers and a polished top, low enough to display a pair of those truly horrendous vases of which the Victorians appear to have been so fond.

GEORGE I WALNUT TALLBOY

IN the early 18th century, the tallboy, or chest on a chest, began to replace the chest on a stand and, by about 1725, had virtually superceded it.

Besides being made fun of, tallboys are made in two parts; the upper chest being slightly narrower than the lower and, although they are inclined to be bulky, this is often minimised visually by means of canted and fluted corners.

Early examples, such as the one illustrated, were veneered in finely grained burr walnut and often sport a sunburst decoration of boxwood and holly at the base, which has the fashionable bracket feet.

George I walnut tallboy   £900

As an added bonus, buyers of these superb pieces of furniture often get a secret drawer in the frieze as well as the brushing slide fitted above the oak lined drawers in the lower section.

A snag: because of the height of these pieces, an Everest style assault has to be launched whenever articles are placed in, or removed from, the upper drawers and this has led to many tallboys being split in half, their top sections being veneered to make two smaller chests. Buyers of early walnut chests of drawers are therefore warned to look twice at those with tops of slightly different colour to that of the rest of the carcase — these could well be split tallboys and worth far less than the chests of drawers they purport to be.

GEORGE III CHEST ON A CHEST

DESPITE the obvious difficulty in reaching the top drawers and the competition from wardrobes and clothes presses, tallboys were made in vast quantities throughout the second half of the 18th century. So common were they, in fact, that George Smith, in his *Household Furniture* observed that the tallboy was an article ". . . of such general use that it does not stand in need of a description".

George III chest on a chest
left: £185
right: £925

As a rule, tallboys were made of mahogany and ranged in quality from rather plain, monolithic but functional pieces to magnificent, cathedral-like specimens with elaborate cornices, fluted pillars flanking the upper drawers, low relief carving on the frieze and fine ogee feet.

The larger picture illustrates a truly magnificent specimen with rococo style handles and a secretaire in the bottom drawer of the upper section.

The other is a more run-of-the-mill chest on a chest with brass loop handles and bracket feet.

LATE 18th CENTURY CHEST ON A CHEST

Late 18th century chest on a chest
left: £110
right: £385

HERE are a couple more chests on chests from the late 18th century.

The example on the right is particularly fine with a bowed front and elegantly splayed feet below a shaped apron. It has ring handles with circular, embossed backplates (which came into fashion about 1770) and is built of finely grained mahogany.

The plinth is omitted in this case to allow the line of the side to drop, uninterrupted, to the floor; possibly more pleasing to the eye than the sometimes jerky-looking effect to be found on many other pieces.

The other piece illustrated is, thanks to friend George Smith, shorter than most, for he declared it to be more convenient ". . . to avoid the disagreeable alternative of getting on to chairs to place anything in the upper drawers".

It is sad that it took furniture designers about 100 years to begin to recognise this; they were obviously just too late to prolong the popularity of the tallboy for I have rarely seen one which was made after about 1820.

GEORGE III CLOTHES PRESS, CIRCA 1760

OAK linen presses fitted with drawers and fielded panel doors were known in Henry VIII's time and, later in the 17th century, most sprouted quantities of the fashionable carving of the period.

There were a few, made of walnut, in the early part of the 18th century but it was not until friend Chippendale spoke up for them in about 1750 that they really came to the fore, proving far more popular than the hanging wardrobe.

Now that we live in an age of fitted cupboards they have been sadly neglected for some time but, fortunately, the quality of craftsmanship employed in their making is now being acknowledged and people are beginning to find room to accommodate them again.

This fine mahogany example dates from 1760 and it has a serpentine front and canted corners decorated with fine Chinese lattice work. The panelled doors open to reveal four sliding oak trays.

If you like the look of this piece but need a good excuse to justify buying it, how about removing the trays (storing them away carefully) and bunging into the space that hideous colour telly which lurks blindly all over the room during its out of use hours?

George III clothes press, circa 1760
£185

REGENCY ROOM

The early years of the nineteenth century saw a great upsurge of classicism in England and the influence of ancient Greek and Roman styles can clearly be seen in the furniture of the period.

They delighted in the use of finely figured foreign woods, as can be seen in the card table of coromandel.

(Courtesy Geffrye Museum)

LATE 18th CENTURY INLAID CLOTHES PRESS

Not only Chippendale, but Hepplewhite, too, championed the cause of the clothes press, stating in his *Guide* of 1788 that he considered them to be ". . . of very considerable consequence as the convenience experienced in their use makes them a necessary piece of furniture".

Most of his designs, beautifully proportioned, had straight dentil cornices and really delicious, finely figured, mahogany panelled doors surrounded by diagonally inlaid satinwood veneers.

The two short and two long drawers are also worthy of note, having inlaid fan designs in their corners and boxwood string inlay.

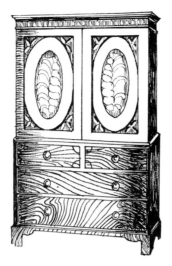

Late 18th century inlaid clothes press
left: £160
right: £110

The secondary illustration represents the variety usually seen in the shops today: plain mahogany with a protective brass strip on the panelled doors and either loop or pressed brass handles.

Like the other, this also has oak sliding trays in the cupboard top since it was considered more desirable to lay clothes flat than to hang them on pegs. This may have been to reduce the need for pressing garments but it was doubtless, too, because the clever dick who invented the coat hanger had not yet come along.

19th CENTURY CLOTHES PRESS

Always end big" being the golden rule in the music halls, who am I to do otherwise?

Here is another gargantuan piece of Victoriana.

This one is of painted pine and, although pieces like it strip quite easily, it is advisable to have this done by a professional with a large caustic tank for, if attempted in the back yard, the sheer size of the task is almost certain to cause enthusiasm to run out with the job half done and you will end up pleading with the dustman to take it away for a quid or two.

These pieces go nicely in a large— and I mean large—kitchen, where they will serve adequately as a larder or a place to stick pots and pans.

19th century clothes press (stripped)
£60

I have seen pieces like this converted into dressers with the aid of a sharp saw and a degree of imagination.

They are usually found in two pieces and the top of the base section is quite large enough to serve as a usable surface once the upper section has been sawn in half. Before attacking the upper half with your saw, however, remove the pediment and trays. The trays can be cut down and made into shelves and the pediment should then be replaced when it can either protrude or be cut down to sit flush with the new depth of the sides.

This may sound rather brutal treatment but the finished effect can be pleasing and very worthwhile, quite apart from the fact that it makes use of a piece which, like the dodo, is unlikely to rise again to a position of prominence in a shrinking world.

Dressers

IN days of old when knights were bold, one of the great status symbols was the size of the family dresser or court cupboard. The king's would stretch from floor to ceiling while those of lesser men would have been correspondingly smaller.

The name "dresser", since you ask, could possibly derive from the fact that its sole original function was to provide a surface on which the food could be dressed before serving, completion of this stage of culinary activity being signalled to ravenous diners by the beating of a drum. Yes, the custom is still practised by seaside landladies, only they sometimes use a gong these days.

(The term Welsh dresser is a 19th century colloquialism for dressers and has no regional derivation beyond a localised preference for certain features.)

The title "court cupboard" dates back to the days when a spade was indeed a spade; it was a board on which cups were displayed in the court, or hall in which court was paid. Since plates and dishes were equally displayed on the thing it could well have been called a cup and plate and dish board but who are we to query the wisdom of our forebears? The point is that it was only later equipped with doors back and sides to become the object which we call a cupboard today.

A mine of useless information, this lad . . .

Call them what you will, all are large pieces of furniture which must be chosen with care for, being of a somewhat rustic nature, they are inclined not to blend too well with their more sophisticated mahogany and walnut town dwelling relatives.

OAK DRESSER CIRCA 1665

DRESSERS developed out of the need for storage for the family table accoutrements and the desire to display such of them as were worth displaying. From the fact that these early dressers were little more than extended side tables without the superstructure of shelves commonly associated with them today we may deduce that few 17th century families had much that was worth displaying in the way of plate or good china.

Oak dresser circa 1665 £600

The dresser above is one of the earliest forms, made of oak with geometrically panelled drawers and baluster front supports with stretchers. Note the brass drop handles character-istic of the period and the back legs—never more than two flat posts—which were never decorated in any way.

The prices commanded by these reflects their age rather than their current popularity for they are usually quite large (up to eight feet long) and take up an enormous amount of room in return for very little storage space.

As an investment, however, I cannot fail to recommend them for there are few pieces of furniture which have survived from this period and any that have cannot possibly fall in value as time goes by.

OAK DRESSER
CIRCA 1670

THIS slightly later dresser (right) maintains the use of geometrically moulded drawer fronts with the characteristically glued-on decoration of split, turned balusters and egg shapes which were frequently made of willow wood dyed to resemble ebony.

These later pieces were generally equipped with three to five baluster supports along the front, without stretchers, but still had only two flat back legs. The timber used in their construction was usually a mellow brown oak, though they are also to be found of elm or fruitwoods and, very rarely, of yew.

Occasionally, dressers of this period may be found to have barley twist legs with stretchers and, although this is rare in early pieces, it seems very popular with 20th century reproducers of the style.

Some pieces may bear marks upon their tops where shelves have rested while fastened to the wall. These would not have been an integral part of the dresser, however, but separate shelf units made, doubtless, for displaying the pewter plates which had replaced the earlier turned wood vessels in common use.

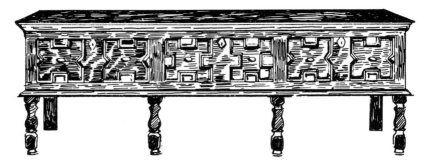

Oak dresser circa 1670 £500

Late 17th century oak dresser £275

LATE 17th CENTURY
OAK DRESSER

IN order to simplify their work and cut costs, cabinet makers of the late 17th century often neglected to produce elaborately turned legs for their products, making do with wavy shapes cut from flat boards instead.

The dresser illustrated above shows the effect of this on the front supports; it has a useful pot board at the base for storing larger cooking pots, crocks and/ or muddy boots.

The drawers have small, turned wooden knobs and Carolean mould - ings, mitred at the corners, to decorate their fronts.

A useful aid to dating furniture from this period is the fact that metal screws were introduced at the end of the 17th century. The trendy, town dwelling cabinet makers were quick to

adopt the screw as a revolutionary (get it?) method of fixing wood but the country craftsmen were slow to make the change, many clinging for years to the old methods ("wooden pegs have been used since the beginning of time, me dear, so I don't see any need to change now. Anyway, if the Good Lord had meant us to use screws he'd have given us stronger fingernails").

But I digress. Before the introduction of screws, the upper parts of dressers were fixed from the top by means of oak pins driven through into the under frame. Screws were inserted from beneath.

The earliest screws were of brass with hand filed threads. From about 1760 the threads were cut on lathes and later, from about 1850, the entire screw was machine made.

EARLY 18th CENTURY
OAK DRESSER

THE fact that most dressers were country made did not necessarily mean that their designs took no account of town styles.

One of the first elaborations on the basic theme saw the addition of a low backboard to the dresser top and a deep, wavy edged apron set below the three drawers. The oak drawers themselves were often crossbanded with walnut but, somehow, the overall effect lacked sophistication and fitted quite comfortably into the average home of the period.

In one of the lean patches which beset my early dealing days, a dresser like this one (over page) was the

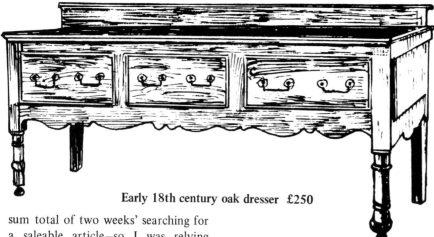

Early 18th century oak dresser £250

sum total of two weeks' searching for a saleable article—so I was relying pretty heavily on it for my wages.

Securing it tightly, or so I thought, to the roofrack of my car, I set off at the crack of a Friday dawn to sell it at Bermondsey Market but, at the traffic lights just down from the Charlie Chaplin pub in the Old Kent Road, I had to brake hard, causing my prize to continue on its way alone. Lacking the power for sustained flight, the dresser landed in the road a couple of feet from my radiator.

Being such an integral part of my future as a dealer, I was obliged to repair it there and then, on the pavement, encouraged by the well chosen comments of half the population of London on its way to work. Fair enough. But then—and this was when I nearly packed up and went home— a rather plump (fat, really) American lady, armed with the usual number of Nikons, and a raucous voice, began taking photographs of me and my dresser, screeching to her equally fat husband to just come here and look at this quaint little English craftsman she had found . . .

18th CENTURY OAK DRESSER CIRCA 1745

DRESSERS, as those of you who have read the introduction will know, were by no means exclusively Welsh products, for variations were introduced in various parts of the country and this one, with cupboards and drawers, was without doubt produced in the north of England.

The cupboard doors were usually panelled and normally plain but better models had a semi-circular shape or, later, ogee mouldings.

Another popular innovation in the early 18th century was the inclusion of a row of small spice drawers set in front of the backboard along the top.

18th century oak dresser circa 1745 £250

All this extra, specialised storage space provided for the kitchen leads me to the conclusion that not only the furniture but the early 18th century taste buds also were developing at an alarming rate, no doubt coinciding with an increase in trade with foreign parts leading to the introduction of delicacies never known in Britain before.

18th CENTURY LANCASHIRE DRESSER

THE ogee feet and brass stamped handles on this dresser place it firmly between the middle and last quarter of the 18th century.

Made of oak with fruitwood banding, it is of better construction than the preceding examples I have given and has a central cupboard behind whose doors is a shelf. Despite these refine-

ments, however, this dresser still has a rather homely, country air about it and has gone about as far as it can go in its development.

By this time, dressers had been ousted from fashionable dining rooms by large side tables or sideboards made of mahogany, the faithful old dressers being relegated to the kitchens or the servants' quarters.

In rural districts, however, dressers continued to hold pride of place in the parlours of farmhouses, positions they richly deserved.

18th century Lancashire dresser £275

EARLY 18th CENTURY OAK DRESSER

IT has been recorded that a few mediaeval cupboard-type dressers had a form of shelving above them but it was not until the beginning of the 18th century that the idea really caught on and became a fully developed, everyday reality.

This dresser, dating from 1730, has fielded and ogee headed panels to the cupboard doors and fielded drawer fronts. (Everyone knows, of course, that fielded is the term used to describe a feature which has the edges bevelled to leave a flat surface—field—in the centre.)

It is topped by shelves with two small cupboards between and is surmounted by a cavetto pediment.

Most early dressers with shelves had no back boards to them (though the example illustrated, of course, does) these often being added later in the century.

One of the reasons for shelves—apart from the obvious one that people were using more cooking utensils than hitherto—was to display the English Delftware which served most families as a substitute for the expensive Chinese porcelain displayed in the homes of people of quality.

Although that smacks to me of an 18th century version of the plastic flower mentality, English Delftware is now held in as high esteem as the Chinese porcelain which it was imitatating, so All's Well that Ends Well . . .

Early 18th century oak dresser £375

CABRIOLE LEG DRESSER CIRCA 1775

IN the late 18th century, when garrulous coachmen were the latest thing in the mass media line, it took a long time for the news to reach our friendly country craftsman that the cabriole leg was the in thing. So long, in fact, that, by the time he had fully accepted it, your sophisticated town dweller had long moved on to other things.

Cabriole leg dresser circa 1775   £375

The drawers in this country-made oak dresser are crossbanded with mahogany and below them is a superbly shaped frieze which is matched by the shaped frieze below the pediment and a row of wavy friezes below the shelves. Still better examples of this style of dresser have shell carving on the knees of the cabriole legs.

The only fault I can find with this elegant dresser lies in the feet of the cabriole legs which, projecting slightly as they do, apparently tended to get in the way of every passing farmer's boot, sustaining considerable damage in the process.

All in all, I think these are rather nice dressers having a delicate air which rather belies their size, though they do tend to crouch a little as though just waiting to spring on unwary passers by.

LATE 18th CENTURY YORKSHIRE DRESSER

THIS is an unusual dresser, mostly referred to as a Yorkshire dresser but, as far as I can ascertain, having no actual roots in that area.

Like the Lancashire dresser referred to earlier, this has ogee feet but the cupboard and drawer arrangement differs, following no set design and apparently being dictated only by the whims of the individual cabinet makers.

A nice feature of the Yorkshire dresser is the timepiece which dominates the super-structure and, presumably, the kitchen in which it stands. It resembles the upper half of a longcase clock as it smiles out from beneath its broken arch pediment and the weights are concealed in the cupboard below.

A fine eighteenth century stripped pine dresser with a nicely shaped frieze.

This early seventeenth century court cupboard is inlaid with bogwood and holly.

Late 18th century Yorkshire dresser £425

Being the centre of culinary activity, the dresser would seem the logical object to be wedded to the kitchen clock as an aid to mealtime punctuality.

This idea has been adopted by manufacturers of modern gas and electric cookers who seem to incorporate clocks more for their decorative than their practical value; often placing them in exactly the best position to be obscured by cooking pots or steam.

OAK AND ELM DRESSER CIRCA 1760

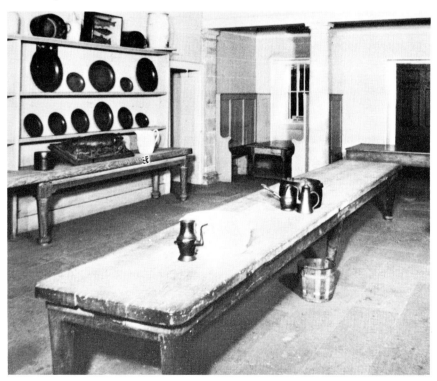

The mid - eighteenth century kitchen at Kedleston Hall, Derbyshire (courtesy of the National Trust).

Oak and elm dresser circa 1760 £375

THIS slightly more elaborate dresser has a baseboard which gives the impression that it travels around with its own section of flooring and that its removal will leave a gaping hole through to the cellar. Don't worry.

In true country style, it is made of both oak and elm, the latter wood being used in places where its attractive figuring will show to best advantage, and it has a pleasantly shaped frieze below the drawer section with fret cut supports for the open shelves.

If you discover a dresser whose top board appears to be lower than you would expect, don't run away with the idea that it was custom made for a short housewife. The explanation lies in the fact that, most old farmhouses having damp floors, a frugal farmer who owned the piece in the past has probably got fed up with the baseboard rotting in his kitchen and removed it altogether.

This naturally reduces the value of such a piece but could be useful if you are short of a few pounds (sterling) or inches, come to that.

LATE 18th CENTURY OAK DRESSER

I HAVE included this dresser for two reasons only; it is of excellent quality and has a practical design which wastes no space anywhere.

The snag lies in its size (up to eight feet long) and it seems such a shame that the ideal kitchen of today is far too small to take pieces such as this for, no matter how much many housewives would like a dresser, it is simply too big even to contemplate.

This one is made of oak and has a dentil cornice below the pediment which often has a fret cut frieze adopted from the fashionable Chippendale style bookcases.

Late 18th century oak dresser £475

This one comes complete with brass loop handles and key escutcheons. It stands on bracket feet and, because of its length, has an additional support in the centre.

It is not only the width, but the height too, which excludes these superb pieces from most households. Which leads me to say that if you are ever considering buying a large piece, always measure the height of your ceilings before parting with money. I had the unfortunate experience recently of buying a magnificent grandfather clock which, standing benignly in my lounge, would have been a constant source of joy. It is now standing in the loo; the only room in the house with a high enough ceiling.

So anyone using the w.c. in my abode will always emerge armed with the useful knowledge that it takes just so long . . .

LATE 18th CENTURY PINE DRESSER

THIS is one of the simpler dressers made in the late 18th century of pine or, occasionally, fruitwood.

It consists of three drawers set atop four plain, square legs and surmounted by a superstructure of open shelves.

A while ago, the local Conservative Association were updating the image of their premises and I noticed a few odds and ends piled against the side of the building and obviously discarded.

In my role as the Friendly Neighbourhood Antique Dealer I was morally obliged to take a quick look just in case anything was worth retrieving before all was lost forever in the depths of the local tip. As I expected, there was little of any use thrown away except—you guessed it—an old pine dresser, heavily disguised with paint (True Blue, naturally.)

A word with the local Agent led to a few pounds being donated to Party funds and the dresser being heaved on to my long suffering roofrack. Since it was too big for me to strip, I popped it round to a friend with a large caustic tank.

"Straightforward enough," said he, "ready in a week." The outcome was a plaintive telephone call every day

Late 18th century pine dresser (stripped) £180

saying "Every time I strip off a coat of blue paint, there's another bloody coat underneath."

Whether or not it was a yearly ritual to paint everything blue as an aid to Party morale, I don't know, but I dread to think of the amount of Party funds spent on blue paint each year.

I wonder if the Labour Party paint their dressers red?

VICTORIAN PINE DRESSER

IF we are to judge by the relics which are to be found today, it would seem that the Victorians were not over fond of producing dressers; cabinet makers preferring to manufacture the more prestigious sideboards and cabinets with more flamboyantly decorative superstructures.

Victorian Pine dresser (stripped) £110

I suspect that the birth of the industrial age caused them to concentrate on the more sophisticated aspects of their craft, considering the humble dresser far too plain and simple an object to warrant the use of their valuable time and machinery. There were, however, a few firms situated at High Wycombe who specialised in making traditional English furniture which had been slightly modified to take advantage of the new, mass production methods and this piece doubtless originated there.

Most of the Victorian dressers that I have seen are either stained or painted—and painted—and painted, though oak made a small comeback later in the period.

Although pieces such as this have little to recommend them aesthetically, they have a certain humble charm and at least fulfil the function for which they were designed while still being of a size to fit into most modern kitchens.

LATE 19th CENTURY OAK DRESSER

Late 19th century oak dresser £70

HERE is an example of a style of furniture which was completely ignored until a few years ago when the earlier pieces became scarce and, consequently, too expensive for the average pocket.

That is not to say that the earlier pieces all fell apart; it is simply that, as more and more people recognise the beauty and investment potential of antiques, fewer and fewer goods find their way on to the market and interest is forced to turn increasingly to later pieces of furniture or, as a final resort, to reproductions of the sought-after styles.

This piece, though I shouldn't say it, looks rather better in the drawing than it does in the flesh. This is because it is nearly always made of a near black oak, which does not do justice to the Elizabethan style of carving and gives it a somewhat funereal appearance overall.

Somewhere underneath all that stain and gunge, however, can be found a nicely grained wood which, with the application of a certain amount of wax and elbow grease produces a fine mellow colour.

OAK DRESSER, 1918

HERE is a 1918 Heal and Sons "Cottage Furniture" Special which, as the catalogue so accurately points out ". . . is always eminently serviceable and has a simple dignity of its own."

If you find its eminent serviceability and simple dignity disagreeable, however, the catalogue hastens to point out that ". . . economy has been studied everywhere, except at the expense of sound construction."

And soundly constructed these certainly were. Almost indestructible, evidently, for I have seen dressers of this kind in secondhand shops in just about every back street in the land. (I've been everywhere man.)

Oak dresser, 1918 £25

That is the present price; in 1918 it was £23. 19s. 6d, complete with washable drawer curtains, the carcase being made of plain, unpolished oak or, at a slightly higher price, oiled, waxed or fumed to any shade.

About this time, Heal's were also producing reproductions of the Jacobean style I referred to in the second example, these priced at the princely sum of £25.

Which would enable the young married couple of 1918 to show a modest profit on their purchase if they were to part with it now after 55 years of loyal service.

MID VICTORIAN ROOM

After the austere elegance of the Regency period came the cluttered opulence of the Victorians.

Flowing lines and rich colours abound, the cabriole leg returns and rococo carving once more comes into its own.

This was the age of industrious domesticity and the ladies of the land proudly displayed the fruits of their labours in the shape of petit point cushions, and woolwork pole screens.

(Courtesy Geffrye Museum)

92

ELIZABETHAN COURT CUPBOARD

**Elizabethan court cupboard £425
Victorian reproduction £55**

THE following six articles include a variety of buffets, court cupboards and tridarns most of which are extremely rare and unlikely to be found in your friendly neighbourhood junk shop.

All geniune pieces in these categories are expensive but they were reproduced in vast quantities throughout the 19th century and these reproductions are usually of good quality and in good condition owing to the Victorian mania for permanence and solidity.

This is a court cupboard—a three tiered form of sideboard—which uses the name cupboard in its original sense of cup board and which has richly carved bulbous supports at the front and flat supports at the back.

As a rule, they have two drawers, one below the centre shelf with deep gadrooning, and another below the top, both used for storing knives and spoons (forks not being in general use until the end of the 17th century).

More exotic examples will be found to have front supports carved to represent fantastic animals, though these are usually confined to the genuine articles. The oldest of these date from the Elizabethan era (1559-1603) and are usually less than four feet high, their three shelves being used for displaying the family plate on festive occasions.

EARLY 17th CENTURY OAK CUPBOARD

AS can be seen, this is the logical successor to the court cupboard. It has a splay fronted enclosed cupboard below the top and is often referred to today as a credence cupboard.

Like the court cupboard, it has drawers below the top and the middle

**Early 17th century oak cupboard £725
Victorian reproduction £85**

shelf and these operate on runners set in the carcase. The bulbous front supports remain and the corbels (bits that stick out at the top) are carved with grotesque lion masks.

Apart from oak, these may be found to be made of walnut, though the interior is usually still of oak, and vary from being quite plain to sporting exotic carving and marquetry decoration and another, similar variety has either one large or three small cupboards set straight across the upper stage, the doors often being recessed and set between wide, straight mouldings.

The base of the piece illustrated has a chequered pattern of ebony and holly—the favourite decoration of the period.

JAMES I OAK CUPBOARD

ANOTHER step forward sees the base section of the piece enclosed and fitted with cupboard doors to match those at the top.

This particular one is a really super example with masses of vigorous carving and base supports in the form of winged griffins.

The baluster supports on these slightly later cupboards were, as a rule, much finer than hitherto—sometimes disappearing altogether—being replaced by a pendant post resting against the front of the cupboard.

As the 17th century wore on, they tended to become much wider than their height and their decoration grew

A particularly fine, early seventeenth century oak court cupboard on bun feet.

progressively plainer. Although still produced in country districts, cupboards of this type were being ousted from fashionable dining rooms by the more sophisticated walnut or lacquered furniture.

The thing to remember concerning these pieces is the fact that their primary function was to impress. Nobody cared too much how practical they were and this is just as well, for they take up an incredible amount of space in comparison with the storage facilities they offer.

James I oak cupboard £1,250
Victorian reproduction £125

17th CENTURY OAK TRIDARN

HAVING filled in the first and second stages of the court cupboard, what was the enterprising cabinet maker to do? Just what he did; put another stage on top.

Although made all over the country, these proved particularly popular in Wales where they received the name Cwpwrdd Tridarn which, as any student of Welsh will tell you, means three stage cupboard.

Made of oak, they were found, as a rule, in the country districts where the design remained virtually unchanged for about a century.

It was a nice custom at the time to give one of these as a wedding present (though God help the young couple who received 15 tridarns, four pop-up toasters and half-a-dozen steam irons to start them on their married lives) and many will be found bearing the initials of the happy pair and the date of their nuptials.

17th century oak tridarn £500
Victorian reproduction £110

But beware! Victorian manufacturers of reproduction furniture sometimes took their work so seriously that they would carve in a reproduction date as well. If the date was one notable in the history of the country, so much the better and 1666 seems to have been a particularly popular choice with greatly enhanced selling power. Doubtless causing many a gullible purchaser to get his fingers burned. . .

LATE 17th CENTURY OAK CUPBOARD

AS I have already mentioned, cupboards tended to become plainer as their development progressed and this one has hardly any ornamentation beyond the turned pediments below the frieze which, occasionally, had a wisp of foliated scroll carving.

The cupboard doors in the lower section are divided into an arrangement of one horizontal and two vertical

Late 17th century oak cupboard £250

panels, which is typical of 17th century furniture, and the doors on the upper section are fielded.

tally genuine pieces should be open to the floor inside the bottom cupboard, which should contain a single shelf.

The doors are supported on butterfly hinges which would have been the work of a locksmith who, in the 17th century, was an entirely new breed of man, all work of this nature formerly being carried out by the blacksmith who was rarely capable of more than simple forging.

MID 18th CENTURY OAK CUPBOARD

THIS rather plain 18th century oak cupboard has its roots firmly planted in the previous century.

The cupboard doors are fielded and panelled in the old style and hang on rather bulky, wrought iron H hinges. Below these, the upper pair of drawer fronts are dummies, to allow extra hanging space, though the lower pair are usually genuine enough.

Mid 18th century oak cupboard £110

These cupboards may have up to three shelves, for the storage of food or linen, or were sometimes left open for hanging clothes or sides of bacon. I have seen them put to a number of uses, none of which involved sides of bacon.

Actually, these are not overpriced, possibly because they are rather plain and unexciting but they are nonetheless well made and, if you can spare the room to house one, it should prove a good investment.

Gaming Tables

THE British people are inveterate gamblers and, although the size of the football pools companies and the numbers of betting shops to be found are indications of this, the majority of modern gamblers have nothing on their predecessors.

Well before the introduction of playing cards, in the 15th century, proficiency at chess, backgammon and dice was considered to be an essential part of the education of anyone intending to take his place in society. Indeed, all forms of gaming were so popular that *The Complete Gamester* was felt to be almost compulsory reading and, in the edition of 1674, we find the declaration ". . . he who in company should appear ignorant of the game in vogue would be reckoned low bred and hardly fit for conversation." Since there were, at that time, dozens of games widely played, including glecko, primero, ombre, picquet, basset, quadrille, commerce and loo, to name but a few, there must have been a considerable

number of people wandering about with inferiority complexes.

And another thing. People in society rarely messed about with gambling for loose change; in many of the higher gaming establishments, the dice were rarely thrown for less than £100 a throw and, in a letter to an acquaintance, the Countess of Sutherland complained mildly of her husband's habit of gambling £5,000 a night on basset which, for the uninitiated, is an old Venetian game, similar to faro (as played in all the best saloons in America's Wild West) in which bets are made on the order of appearance of certain cards.

Early games were played on marked boards (as chess and draughts) which were placed either on the floor or on a table. Towards the end of the 17th century, however, the business of losing a fortune was civilised somewhat by the introduction of beautifully made gaming tables specifically designed for players of particular games.

WILLIAM AND MARY CARD TABLE

THIS is one of the first tables to have been made specifically for the playing of card games and it was introduced during the William and Mary period (1689–1695).

The circular folding top is veneered in finely grained walnut and stands upon six legs, of which the two at the rear are pivoted in order that the table, when not in use, may be stood flat against a wall. Rarer examples of this type of table have rectangular tops but they employ the same system of folding away.

Legs are either tapered or turned and they are united, just above the feet, with flat, shaped stretchers, and, as a rule, the frieze will be found to contain small drawers for the storage of cards and chips, and doubtless for early equivalents of that well known brand of chewing gum which is such a miraculous aid to concentration.

William and Mary card table £625

The table illustrated and described above is the one most usually seen, but I have found examples in this style decorated with arabesque marquetry, though these will cost around twice as much as their plainer relations.

There was a smaller card table made during the same period which was designed for the two handed game of picquet. This had a square top with flaps folding outward from the centre and was supported on a central column with three scrolled feet. These tables are now extremely rare, however, and their high prices tend to make other tables seem very reasonable.

QUEEN ANNE CARD TABLE

THE cabriole leg, with its bulk and strength disguised in the graceful flow of line, was introduced during the early part of the 18th century and had a far reaching effect on furniture design from that time onward.

Card players in particular felt the benefit of this innovation since they were no longer obliged to negotiate a framework of stretchers each time they sat at, or rose from, their game. (Doubtless, too, better players appreciated the fact that they were now free to place kicks accurately on the shins of partners guilty of tactical errors without the risk of hitting a stretcher and booting the entire table across the floor.)

Queen Anne card table £575

As regards playing cards: earliest examples were made of either parchment or fabric stiffened with varnish, and it was not until Tudor times that paper was used for the purpose. As a rule, backs were plain but the faces, apart from being marked with the suit and number, were decorated.

By 1628, foreign imports of playing cards were disturbing home manufacturers to the extent that Charles I was persuaded to grant British producers of cards the protection of a Royal Charter. In 1712, gaming having become a national mania, the *Guardian* felt obliged to denounce women gamesters, declaring that "Nothing wears out a fine face like the vigils of the card table . . ." No doubt this prompted Queen Anne to impose a tax of sixpence on each pack, to be indicated on the ace of spades. This is useful in the dating of packs of cards for, apart from bearing the cypher of the reigning mon-

arch, the indication of the amount of tax paid varied frequently, thus allowing fairly accurate estimates of dates.

GEORGE I CARD TABLE

AS the design of gaming tables progressed, tops tended to become square in shape, but with circular projections on the corners which were dished to hold candlesticks and which also had oval wells for money and chips.

The legs became progressively bolder, the earlier spade and club feet giving way to lions' paws or ball and claw designs. In about 1720, mahogany superceded walnut as the most widely used wood in the construction of gaming tables, though, occasionally, more exotic woods, such as laburnum, were used.

Prior to this time, carving had generally been rather limited—perhaps a shell motif on the knee—but with the introduction of the harder mahogany, more intricate designs, such as lion masks, were added and hairy lions' paw feet employed, accounting for the denomination "lion period" often being applied to early Georgian furniture.

George I card table £525

In the early days, stones or shells were widely used as token money for games of skill and chance and it was not until the 17th century that chips as we know them were manufactured, these being small discs of tortoiseshell, bone, ivory, mother-of-pearl or of metals such as pewter and brass. Naturally, the more salubrious gaming establishments used more exotic chips, these often being made of precious metals, exquisitely chased and decorated.

GEORGE II CARD TABLE

CARD tables with square corners were first made around 1730, remaining popular throughout the Georgian period—no doubt to suit the current fashion for square shaped candlesticks. As time passed, the cabriole legs became finer again, accepting a rococo influence around 1750, when scroll feet were all the rage.

A variety of shaped tops was also introduced during the 1750s, in keeping with the rococo tradition, and the most popular of these had a serpentine shape whose elegance was acclaimed by William Hogarth in his *Analysis of Beauty,* 1753, when he set the world alight by declaring that a curved line was more graceful than a straight one (would you believe!).

Card tables were also, during this period, enhanced by the addition of fine friezes whose mouldings often took the form of delicate scroll or foliage designs.

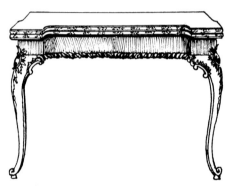

George II card table £450

The popularity of gaming continued unabated, eventually causing the more famous coffee and chocolate houses to develop into gambling clubs, their original, and often highly intellectual, characters being lost forever.

With stakes as high as they were at that time, the one man not to be envied was the Groom Porter whose duties, apart from seeing that the King's Lodgings were adequately furnished with card and dice tables, also entailed the settling of disputes arising out of gaming.

GEORGE III CARD TABLE

BY the 1770's, gambling had reached such a peak that King George III felt it necessary to forbid the playing of cards in any of the Royal Palaces and Horace Walpole, that indefatigable commentator on the fashions of his time, is reported to have remarked that the gaming at Almacks, where young blades were losing as much as £15,000 in a night, was ". . . worthy of the decline of the Empire".

George III card table £425

"Low" tables were introduced at this time with a view to encouraging people to play for lower stakes, but to be seen at one was held by the arbiters of fashion to be somewhat infra dig, and Lady Mary Cooke observed that low tables in a house were ". . destined to bring out odds and ends that nobody thinks of inviting when better are to be had".

Card tables themselves took on a new lease of life, however, with designs by such notables as Adam, Sheraton, and Hepplewhite raising them to fresh heights of elegance.

This fine table from about 1775 is of satinwood, with slender tapered legs and it is decorated with festoons of flowers, the carved rococo scrollwork being quite out of fashion by this time.

The inside of the folding top should be lined with green baize and, although the wells for candles and counters have been omitted, this should not prove unaccommodating for the average 20th century buyer.

In part, the popularity of this style springs from the fact that, folded shut, it serves adequately as a pier table.

REGENCY CARD TABLE

ALTHOUGH the Prince of Wales, who was later Prince Regent and finally King George IV, extolled the virtues of games of cards, it would appear that the popularity of the pastime had waned somewhat, for 19th century cabinet makers were producing far fewer card tables than their predecessors.

Most Regency card tables are of rosewood and the tremendous variations of price which may be observed directly reflect the extent, or absence, of the brass inlay and the fineness of the base.

The example I have chosen here dates from 1815 and its fine proportions and beautiful inlay work mark it as one of the better pieces of its kind. The folding top of this table is supported on a central column which, in turn, rests upon a shaped platform with four nicely shaped splay feet terminating in brass castors.

More exotic bases are in the form of a lyre and have spavin legs (which is a most uncomplimentary term to describe what is, after all, quite an elegant shape).

Regency card table £240

LATE REGENCY CARD TABLE

ALL right, all right. The prices of the card tables I have selected so far have all been somewhat on the high side—that is just one of the unhappier facts of life. From here on, prices are rather more reasonable. . .

Late Victorian card table £115

This elegant fellow dates from the early 19th century and is made of mahogany with ebony and satinwood inlay with a crossbanded top.

The nicely fluted legs are quite fine when they are compared with those of some later Victorian varieties and,

all in all, it is a good serviceable table which does not sacrifice too much in the way of looks for the sake of practical considerations.

Most card tables are, as everyone knows, baize lined and it is surprising how frequently this material needs replacing if the table is to retain its smart good looks.

Baize can be bought quite reasonably for under £1 per square yard and it comes in widths of 36 and 72 inches. Personally, I find Evo Stick one of the best adhesives for attaching the baize to the top but be careful to use the adhesive sparingly, otherwise it tends to seep into and even through the baize, leaving a hard, ugly patch.

Just another tip: cut the material about an inch larger all round than the area to be covered and trim it to size with a sharp Stanley knife when the adhesive is dry.

I always get the feeling that card tables really appreciate being fitted with a new lining. When the job is finished, they seem to sit with a smug sort of glow about them, just begging to be played on.

WILLIAM IV CARD TABLE

THIS card table is the logical progression from the one before last, the Regency example, and it dates from about 1830.

The folding top is of a similar shape to that of its forebear but it is not quite as elegant and the base, with its paw feet, owes more to the whims of fashion than to classical design standards. The central column, usually

William IV card table £115

A superior pair of late eighteenth century satinwood card tables, delicately inlaid with various woods, on square tapering legs with spade feet.   £5,500

round, has here become more flamboyant with a flurry of leaf carving at the base.

These tables, of either rosewood or mahogany, are nearly always of good quality and represent good value for money.

I was walking round the Lanes, the antique shop district of Brighton, one bitterly cold day when trade was bad when I came across four dealers playing cards round a table similar to this in the shop belonging to one of them.

Instead of playing for money, they were gambling odds and ends of old stock—"I'll raise you a trivet and a Victorian bottle"—"I'll raise two odd silver spoons and a broken writing slope" and so on. In terms of actual cash, these were fairly high stakes and, as often happens, the stakes escalated steadily as the game progressed until, when two of the players each had good hands, the stakes rose to an Edwardian bureau against the card table on which the game was being played.

Three kings and a pair of queens gave the game to Mr.Edwardian Bureau who promptly folded up the game, and the table, carrying both back to his premises a few doors down the street.

EARLY VICTORIAN CARD TABLE

Early Victorian card table £120

IN the same way that teak might be described as *the* wood of the mid 20th century and "Scandinavian" the

style, so might burr walnut and rococo be described as the fashionable combination of the mid 19th century.

This card table is one of the earlier Victorian pieces which were, as a rule, of a high quality which was not, unfortunately, maintained for long.

We see that the central column has diminished to some extent and, in some cases, has virtually disappeared, giving way to a quadruple display of shaped legs with scroll feet.

The folding top is nicely shaped and is usually inlaid with boxwood.

You may find that the legs of a table of this type have become loose and appear to present a problem of accessibility for the re-gluing process.

Simply flip the table over and you will find that the decorative end of the central column will unscrew, revealing that the legs are dove-tailed into the base. Having exposed the joints, it is a relatively simple matter to tap the legs out, clean all joined surfaces and re-glue the legs in position. Great care must be taken, however, to remove no wood from the joints during the cleaning, otherwise the legs will never re-glue securely.

No screws or clamps are needed to hold the legs in position while the glue sets; simply turn the table the right way up and the weight of the piece will ensure good, tight joints.

LATE VICTORIAN CARD TABLE

THIS later Victorian stretcher card table comes in three qualities: good, bad, and why did I bother? These qualities are instantly recognisable by means of the woods employed which, in the same order, are burr walnut, plain walnut and ebonised pinewood, which, if stripping is attempted, yields a black goo of the consistency of poor quality toffee.

The burr walnut pieces are usually inlaid with boxwood, some even sporting a bunch of inlaid flowers, and they are of fairly sound construction, as are those of plain walnut.

The ebonised models are really not worth bothering with unless you happen to have a taste for badly made black furniture (dealers call it Funeral Wood).

Burr walnut card table £70

Tables of this type are opened by rotating the top horizontally through 90 degrees and folding the baize lined top flap over to lie on the section of frame thus exposed.

One of the main disadvantages of a table of this kind is the return of the stretchers—a feature which had long since been recognised as an encumbrance. This ensures that third and fourth players spend the duration of their game sitting with legs stretched wide apart and are liable to walk home bow legged.

LATE 19th CENTURY
CARD TABLE

THERE were any number of inventions and innovations which sprouted during the second half of the 19th century, most of which got no further than a filing cabinet in the Patents Office.

This little envelope table was one that got away and, having been produced, proved very popular indeed. Like many of the other pieces of its period, it is to be found in a number of variations and the best of these are made of brown mahogany with boxwood string inlay and, occasionally, superb marquetry flowers. Another variant is plainer, of red mahogany, with shaped legs in contrast to the plain legs and spade feet of the brown example.

Late 19th century card table £60

This table has one drawer below the top, which is opened by slightly moving it to one side. This action operates a lever which raises one of the leaves to allow the fingers to lift all four flaps and fold them back to form a baize lined square.

The piece of Victorian gadgetry which appealed to me most of all was the nice little upright piano which, with the slip of a catch and the pull of a lever, converted into, wait for it, a double bed! Ideal for the restless sleeper who needs a quick bit of Rimsky-Korsakov to help get in the mood for sleep.

EDWARDIAN
CARD TABLE

HAD you walked into Heal and Sons, Tottenham Court Road, at the turn of the century, you might have bought one of these "Walnut and Ebonised Corner Card Tables Lined with Cloth" for the princely sum of £4 15s. 0d. (that's £4.75 for those who have forgotten what real money looked like) and, up until recently, that is what your friendly neighbourhood junk man would have asked you to pay for the same item from his stock.

Although pieces like this are, fortunately, not in fashionable demand in this country, they are, even more luckily, being exported in sufficient numbers to cause the price to rise above that which anyone with sense would dream of paying.

I, personally, would not accept one of these as a gift for, although they adequately fulfil the function for which they were designed, they tend to sit in otherwise pleasant rooms like inkblots on love letters.

If I seem unkindly disposed towards furniture such as this, it is because I have a sort of Judas relationship with the furniture in my own house; I tend to regard each piece as a friend but, being a dealer at heart, I can never totally ignore a good offer.

Although I would never part with a certain number of the pieces in my

home, I tend to sell and replace some of the others fairly frequently. This can be inconvenient at times, particularly when I go to retrieve something which I had put in a safe place only to find that the "safe place" was sold a week ago.

Edwardian card table £25

LATE 18th CENTURY
GAMES TABLE

DESPITE the fact that games such as chess and backgammon had been popular for a few hundred years by the time playing cards were introduced, articles of furniture designed specifically to accommodate the playing of these ancient games were not developed until some time after the introduction of card tables.

Chess and backgammon tables may now be found in about the same numbers as card tables, particularly those dating from the end of the 18th to the late 19th century. Although a few earlier pieces do exist, it was during this period that tables such as these really came into their own, often being combined with a workbox, and it was Sheraton who took such a delight in the idea of variable purpose furniture that he often designed pieces with as many as six possible uses.

This 18th century piece, in mahogany, is an absolute delight; the centre section of the top is leather covered, for writing, and it reverses to reveal a chessboard, often with small inlaid rectangles of cribbage score boards along either side.

Below the top is a two-part well, with a sham drawer front, designed for

Late 18th century games table £450

the playing of tric trac—a complicated form of backgammon in which pegs as well as pieces are used.

REGENCY GAMES TABLE

HERE is another superb piece of furniture from the Regency period, which has even more uses than my previous example.

Made of rosewood, this little table is surmounted by a pierced brass gallery and has fine scroll brass inlay on the drawer. The legs, which I find particularly attractive, have the splay feet and brass claw castors which are typical of the period.

Apart from having a top adjustable for reading and writing, this piece has a slide marked out for chess and, lower down, a sliding work bag for the storage of needlework and sewing.

Regency games table £525

102

Workboxes, like chess tables and some people, were late developers and, as a rule, followed slavishly the fashions of the day.

In Tudor times, the implements for embroidery and other needlework being highly prized since they had to be imported from Italy and Holland, were kept in small chests or stools with hinged lids.

It was not until about 1650 that knitting needles and other accessories were manufactured on a commercial scale in this country, housewives prior to that time having to put up with tools of their own (or their husbands') manufacture.

EARLY VICTORIAN GAMES TABLE

THIS is a good combined games and work table of early Victorian (about 1845) manufacture and design which has unfortunately (or, fortunately, depending on whether you are buying or selling) almost tripled in price over the past few years. It is still, however, well worth its money in my opinion.

Early Victorian games table £160

The octagonal top is on U-shaped supports and the small centre column extends down to the platform base and its scroll feet. The exterior of the well (between the U-supports) is finished with woolwork, doubtless the result of many hours of work by an early owner, though this may be found to have been replaced with velvet.

Reading and writing are not provided for this time, the chessboard

top lifting to reveal a cloth or paper covered tray which is divided into a number of compartments and small boxes intended for silks and sewing materials.

Below this tray is the well, in which unfinished work would normally be kept, and wool. There is normally no provision for chess pieces in workboxes of this kind, but there are any number of small Victorian boxes available which adequately fill the bill.

VICTORIAN GAMES TABLE

Victorian games table £95

ABOUT ten years after the previous table was produced came this piece which, with its stretcher base and cabriole legs, was more in keeping with the rococo style fashionable at the time.

Usually made of burr walnut with superb figuring, though sometimes of rosewood, this is a particularly good table for displaying bits and pieces. It has a double top, however, which lifts and turns to the side to form an extended surface for writing or playing cards and this is inlaid with black and natural squares for chess.

These pieces are of good quality but, walnut is, unfortunately, particularly attractive to the palate of every passing woodworm grub and therefore should be checked over fairly regularly for the signs of fresh dust which indicate that you are entertaining these unwelcome guests.

Another slight disadvantage in some households is the sliding bag below the fitted drawer. This tends to be used at first for its proper purpose, the storage of wool, and then it gradually becomes filled with other odds and ends until it contains as much junk as the average lady's handbag.

LATE VICTORIAN GAMES TABLE

THE moving fabric of time unfolds (as Walt Disney might say) and, a few years later, we find that the economics of factory productions have begun to mean rather more to manufacturers than meticulous workmanship and elegant design.

This workbox fulfils the same functions in the same ways as the previous examples but what a difference in quality of manufacture and design!

Late Victorian games table £60

As a result of the low standard of craftsmanship tolerated by some manufacturers at this time, many pieces such as this—built on a central pedestal with a tripod base—have become badly damaged around the feet. (Though to be fair, the enduring popularity of this general style has ensured that most surviving pieces have stood up to a considerable amount of usage).

When buying, therefore. look carefully for damage in that area and also for a difference in the colour of the wood of the top and the base. Any variation here usually means that the piece has been restored to service by marrying the top of one piece to the bottom of something else and this

always detracts from the value.

I must say, though, that I can see nothing whatever wrong with this method of salvaging otherwise irreparable furniture provided that the object of the exercise is not to mislead. It does, after all, save for succeeding generations two otherwise useless pieces of furniture which might have been discarded.

EDWARDIAN GAMES TABLE

ALTHOUGH the bulk of workboxes and games tables were made between, roughly, 1775 and 1875, there were a few made during the final years of the century and during the Edwardian period.

Most of these "tail end Charlies" were made in an incredible, pseudo-Gothic style and are best ignored, but those made in the style of the late 18th century are well worth buying. The one illustrated is of mahogany, with boxwood string inlay and square tapered legs with a shelf at the base.

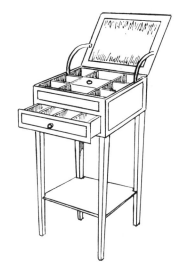

Edwardian games table £40

The hinged chessboard top rises to reveal the sewing compartments as might be expected but the fitted drawer has a small surprise to offer, being spring loaded to pop out when a small brass button is pressed in the rim at the back of the piece.

Although a wee bit small for the enthusiastically gadget minded sempstress of today, this is a very pleasant piece of furniture and should prove quite adequate for those whose needle-

craft is confined to replacing the occasional button or darning the odd sock.

19th CENTURY GAMES TABLE

THERE were any number of tables produced during the 19th century which were designed for nothing more than the playing of chess and which can be bought almost anywhere for under £40.

Here is a rather better one.

19th century games table £250

Structurally much the same as any other table, it is the top which raises this one out of the rut, being of beautiful, fine grained Welsh slate. There have been some superb effects obtained through the use of this slate for it comes in a variety of shades and colours including grey, black, blue, purple and green and the craftsmanship employed on its use always seems to have been of the absolute best.

Being heavy and soft, slate has the unfortunate habit of shattering when it is dropped and, in consequence, relatively few of these tables have survived—hence the high price.

I was pleased to hear, however, that slate is making a comeback as a decorative material, partly, it seems, because of its resistance to much of the corrosive sludge which we euphemistically call "fresh air" and partly because it really is a beautiful material which obtains a fine gloss easily with the administration of wax polish.

GEORGE III COACHING TABLE

ALTHOUGH this was not designed as a card table, I have no hesitation in including it here, since it serves admirably for that purpose and folds away conveniently when not in use.

Actually, it is a George III coaching table, made of mahogany and designed to be carried on the back of milord's coach in order to provide a more civilised platform than God's earth for the game pies when pangs of hunger struck in mid journey.

After use, the top, which is hinged in the centre, is allowed to fold down by releasing a catch underneath and bringing the sides together.

An unusually complex gaming table attributed to Abraham Roentgen, on superbly carved cabriole legs with grotesque masks on the feet, circa 1730.

George III coaching table £75

If this seems a little pricey for what it is, remember that antiques bought at the right price are a good investment and, perhaps, ask yourself how much your actual 1973 picnic table in tubular aluminium and surfaced hardboard is going to fetch in 100 years' time!

A fine George II burr walnut card table on superb cabriole legs with ball and claw feet.

104

GAMES
BOXES

WHILE on the subject of gaming tables, I feel I must include at least a couple of games boxes since these date back to the time the very first games were played—board games, that is, and there are early records of some very fine pieces.

At Kenilworth Castle, for example, in 1588, we are told of an ebony box, exquisitely inlaid with ivory and silver, containing chessmen described in the same inventory as being ". . of christall and other stones layed with sylvere, garnished with bears and ragged Stayves."

Another, belonging to Charles I, was set with pearls and precious stones and was equipped with silver chessmen.

The boxes illustrated are not so grand but they have a certain charm of their own.

Both are Victorian and superbly veneered in burr walnut: the card box is embellished with chased gilt brass mounts and ivory cards, the interior being divided for two packs, while the other box has a backgammon and a chess board in the lid and contains boxwood chequers and chessmen with a space for a cribbage board and cards.

Card box (top) £15
Games box (below) £50

Cabinets

ENTION the word "cupboard" and everyone within earshot can be reasonably expected to know what you are talking about. Mention the word "cabinet" and listeners will conjure for themselves pictures of anything from puddings to politicians with something like 50 different pieces of furniture in between.

Cabinets, as pieces of furniture, saw their British beginnings in the 17th century, when designed basically for either specialised storage or display, they were introduced by craftsmen imported from the continent.

It was during the 18th and 19th centuries, however, that cabinets began to achieve a certain importance when they served to meet the needs of a nation obsessed with learning. Everybody it would seem, began to collect

things; coins, shells, fossils, ores, mineral samples, china-and what was the point of amassing vast collections of these wonders without having the means of displaying them for the enjoyment of family and admiring friends?

Cabinets, then, became indispensable, and although most of the earlier examples were imported from Europe, a few were actually made in Britain. Even these, however, were usually made by foreign craftsmen working in British factories and they were commonly attributed to other European countries despite the fact that they were physically made here.

It was only later, from about 1690 that British designers turned their talents toward the creation of cabinets that were of sufficiently British character to be unquestionably attributed to home manufacturers.

EARLY 17th CENTURY FLEMISH CABINET

NECESSITY, to coin a phrase, is the mother of invention, and the pedigree of the cabinet gives no cause to doubt the accuracy of that statement.

The coffer, for centuries the only storage unit available in the home, was too convenient as a parking place for idle members of the family who had first to be removed before access could be gained to its contents. It was inevitable, therefore, that a brighter than average woodworker should hit on the idea of screwing down the lid of his coffer and fixing doors on the front so that people or objects need not be removed from the top every time something was needed from within.

Following complaints that it was both inconvenient and embarrassingly

Early 17th century Flemish cabinet £2,750

immodest for a lady to crawl about on the floor every time she needed some-

thing from the family chest, the piece was raised on a stand and called a cabinet. Being a fashionable innovation and one which was in demand in the wealthy homes, woodworkers really went to town in displaying their skills and, as a means of raising themselves to a cut above their fellows, many began to call themselves Cabinet Makers.

This, one of the earliest cabinets to be found, is of ebony inset with panels of pietre dure (a composition of fragments of marble and other stones) which are mounted in gilt brass frames.

Ebony cabinets were much sought after in early 17th century England, doubtless following the return of Buckingham from a royal marriage making a trip to Spain during which he found the time to buy a "Spanish Cabinet of Ebony" for the princely sum of £8.

CHARLES II LACQUERED CABINET

TO suit the taste for richly ornamental furnishings current during the late Stuart period, the East India Company imported quantities of lacquered cabinets from the mysterious Orient.

As a rule these were decorated with scenes in high relief, usually in red and green on a black ground (though occasionally on a red ground toward the end of the 17th century) and their designs were sometimes, in the very best examples, embellished with gold and silver additions.

These cabinets have very ornate, hand engraved brass hinges and fittings on the doors which open to reveal numerous small drawers and cupboards. Although they were imported with accompanying lacquered stands, these were usually considered too low for the European taste and were often replaced by superbly carved softwood stands.

Stands made for these cabinets were extraordinarily ornate, with flamboyant carving in the style of the Italian Rennaissance incorporating massive scroll legs, crowns, cupids, eagle heads and acanthus leaves which were carefully silvered or gilded. Later, toward the end of the 17th century and during the first half of the 18th century, the stands, still made by European craftsmen, became less flamboyant and tended toward the French style with its tapered legs and low relief carving.

A late 18th century Dutch marquetry china cabinet profusely decorated with floral sprays.   £1,500

Charles II lacquered cabinet   £2,250

WILLIAM AND MARY CABINET

THIS excellent cabinet comes from the William and Mary period and it is made of walnut decorated with seaweed marquetry which was then at its height of development.

The stand, also decorated with marquetry, has fine, S scroll supports and shaped stretchers with acanthus carved feet and the exterior decoration is continued inside the cabinet itself. This usually contains twelve small drawers set around a central cupboard.

The real feature of pieces such as this is the quality of design and workmanship displayed in the marquetry decoration. The intricate, scroll-like patterns were inspired by A.C.Boulle who used brass and tortoiseshell for his own designs whereas these are executed in either boxwood or holly for the light pattern and darker walnut for the ground.

The two selected veneers were pasted together with paper between them to enable easier separation and the design was placed on the top surface ready for cutting. A fine saw was used to cut out the pattern and the art lay in holding the saw at exactly the right angle to the work so that, when the veneers were parted and pieced together like a jigsaw puzzle, there would be no gaps caused by the thickness of the saw blade.

William and Mary cabinet   £1,100

QUEEN ANNE LACQUERED CABINET

Queen Anne lacquered cabinet £1,000

As the development of the cabinet progressed the base section often became filled with drawers, the upper half retaining its cupboard doors enclosing a series of beautifully made cupboards and small drawers.

This Queen Anne Cabinet indicates the popularity of lacquer work which never entirely fell from grace during the following century and a half, at the end of which it saw a tremendous revival under the Victorians. In the early 18th century, indeed, demand exceeded supply of the genuine oriental work to the extent that it became quite fashionabel for young ladies to take up the craft and even attend classes organised for its teaching.

Despite all efforts, English lacquer work, being of largely amateur execution, was regarded as inferior not only to the genuine article but also to the marquetry and other ornate veneered work which enjoyed current popularity.

Despite its comparitive inferiority much of the English lacquer work was undeniably beautiful and could pass, to the untrained eye, as being of Oriental origin. Look at the borders which, under English hands, tended to degenerate into a series of meaningless blobs and squiggles when compared with the legendary symbolism of Eastern work. Look too, at the comparative lack of vitality and meaning in the figures and animals and do not be misled by the brass hinges which, although on a par with those of Oriental origin, tend to be of heavier construction.

MID 18th CENTURY MARQUETRY VITRINE

IN the early 18th century, Oriental porcelain and Delftware became extremely popular and a need arose for suitably fine cabinets with glazed upper sections in which to display it to its full advantage.

Early styles had straight cornices and doors glazed in half round mouldings, the whole supported on turned legs with stretchers. As taste developed, however, heavy architectural styles in the manner of William Kent became popular, often displaying dentil cornices, and broken-arch pediments, as illustrated below, with fielded panelled doors below the glazed section.

The word vitrine is just another name for a china cabinet, used by some antique dealers in the belief that it puts a few quid on the price. Come to think about it, that is exactly what it does.

The marquetry decoration on this piece is typical of its Dutch style, consisting of naturalistic birds and flowers executed in shaped reserves. Shading of the leaves and flowers was, during the first half of the 18th century, achieved by dipping the veneered shapes part way into hot sand but this later gave way to a method of engraving the shading on to the actual surface of the finished marquetry pattern.

Mid 18th century marquetry vitrine £1,000

CHIPPENDALE PERIOD CABINET ON A STAND, CIRCA 1780

Chippendale period cabinet on a stand £1,000

IT was not long before the heavy, architecturally styled cabinets were recognised as being inappropriate for the display of delicate china and porcelain. They were quickly relegated to the libraries of the nation for the storage of books, their places being taken in fashionable drawing rooms by far more graceful display cabinets such as this one.

Never slow to turn an imported fashion to their advantage, designers such as Chippendale helped to perpetuate the taste for things Oriental by producing fine Chinese-influenced styles incorporating some incredibly delicate fretwork.

The piece above is a particularly fine example of the sort of thing being produced during this period, incorporating a secretaire in the fretted centre drawer.

It was Chippendale's forte to take an established style and use it in his own designs, maintaining the original feeling but overlaying it with his own individual stamp—genius indeed.

LATE 18th CENTURY SHERATON STYLE CABINET

CORNERS of rooms are notoriously difficult to furnish and should really be left uncluttered if not filled with a piece of furniture designed expressly for the purpose.

This nice, late 18th century, figured mahogany corner display cabinet was made in the Sheraton style and it has pleasing curved glazing bars and satinwood decoration.

This particular cabinet, as you will have noticed, is on the expensive side but, thanks to our Edwardian friends who revived late 18th century styles, a good corner display cabinet can be bought for about £140.

These reproductions are made of mahogany decorated with boxwood stringing and have a conche shell inlaid in the cupboard door at the base while the upper door is glazed with a mystical 13 divisions. They have bracket feet and originally were made with swan neck pediments but, as these

Late 18th century Sheraton style cabinet £380

were only fastened with a couple of dowels, many have unfortunately gone astray.

There is also a cheaper cabinet of the same period but of plain mahogany with a straight glazed door which sells at about £50.

So you pays your money and takes your choice.

VERNIS MARTIN CABINET

THIS is a particularly fine china cabinet which really appeals to me. It dates from the Louis Philippe period (1830–1848) when furniture was decidedly flash and is veneered in

A highly carved late 19th century Japanese hardwood cabinet with mother of pearl and ivory decoration. £750

kingwood with fine ormolu mounts. The shape is delicious as are the decorated panels on the lower section which are a 19th century revival of an earlier fashion.

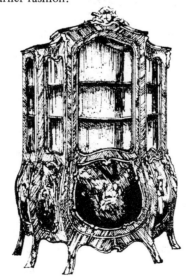

Vernis Martin Cabinet £850

About 1730, Vernis Martin, a French carriage painter, developed along with his three brothers, Guillaume, Julien and Robert, a method of lacquering which was especially suited to taking fine painting. He used many ground colours but his green lacquer proved most popular and brought him such fame that he had the fortune to be patronised by no less a personage than Madame de Pompadour.

Although his first patent granted him a monopoly of japanning in the Chinese style for 20 years, most of the decorations seen today are panels depicting delicate garden scenes and interiors painted in a style after Watteau. Other work consists of a plain ground stippled with gold.

Like the later Oriental lacquer work, that undertaken by any but the masters of the technique is usually inferior though it might still have considerable beauty.

19th CENTURY FRENCH DISPLAY CABINET

THE fashionable likes and dislikes of the Victorians were complex, often conflicting and, at times, altogether confusing; conditions which might have delighted early psychoanalysts but which are guaranteed to destroy the mind of anyone foolish enough to try to rationalise the constant changes.

19th century French display cabinet £265

The piece illustrated above is a superb display cabinet from about 1850. It is made of gilded walnut and has beautiful lines which are emphasised by the slightly exaggerated cabriole legs with their scroll feet. Like a good picture frame, this piece will enhance the beauty of anything placed in it without overly distracting the attention.

There are two main gilding processes; water gilding, which is rather complicated but provides better lustre, and oil gilding which is more commonly found since it is a cheaper and easier process, though the finish obtained by this process is not so fine.

Both methods require a good, carefully prepared ground since the wood alone is never hard or smooth enough. Gesso (a paste of chalk, plaster and and gypsum ground in water) is commonly used for both processes but an alternative preparation of white lead or red ochre ground in oil will be found to be satisfactory for the oil gilding

method. This mixture is applied in thin coats, each being allowed to dry thoroughly before the next is added. When the final coat (about three coats are sufficient) is dry, this ground is prepared and an adhesive applied.

Take my word for it that this is not an easy process, but if you must try it, supplies and advice can be obtained from Windsor & Newton who service most good art shops.

ORIENTAL DISPLAY CABINET

THE mysticism of the Orient has always proved fascinating to Occidentals, particularly the romantic Victorians, whose enthusiasm led department stores to decorate whole floors in a suitably eastern manner.

Oriental display cabinet £150

This 19th century, carved hardwood display cabinet has all the features calculated to endear it to a Victorian mystic, including an air of inscrutability, lots of vigorous carving and a touch of rococo feeling in the shape of the legs—Confucius would have loved it.

The main drawback with pieces such as this is their need for constant attention with a feather duster—all right for the Victorian housewife with her army of servants, but not likely to appeal too strongly to your average working mum these days.

One unique feature of Chinese furniture is the total absence of nails and

screws, all construction being based on a mortice and tenon principal with a limited use of dovetailing and glue—a method of construction which allowed the wood to adapt to severe climatic changes without the article falling to pieces. Another interesting feature is the way in which the pieces were designed to stand flat against a wall or at right angles to it so as to leave floor space clear in the centre of the room.

While we're on the subject of Chinese traditions, remember that, when entertaining guests in your Oriental room, you should place them on your left, facing the door and at the farthest point in the room from it. Now there's a useful piece of information for you, especially if you have been doing it all wrong and wondering why the neighbours have been talking unkindly about you.

EDWARDIAN INLAID MAHOGANY CHINA CABINET

THIS is a typically Edwardian china cabinet which was made in the style of the late 18th century.

Edwardian inlaid mahogany china cabinet £90

It is superbly made of mahogany, with boxwood string inlay and supported on fine, square tapered legs with spade feet. Thankfully, pieces such as this have recently returned to favour for, less than a decade ago, they were fetching about a tenner, and many dealers would not even bother to lift

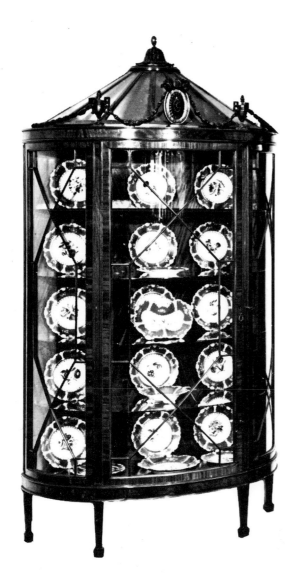
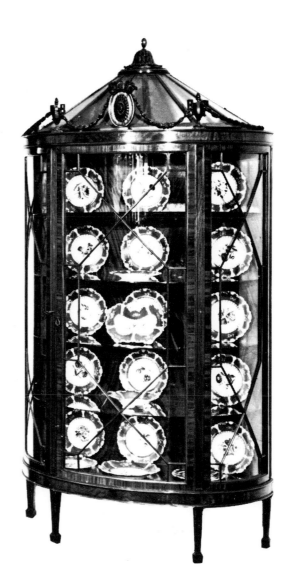

An interesting pair of walnut veneered china cabinets made about 1930 in the Adam style. £1,000

them for such a miserable sum, let alone give them shop room. I used to turn them down by the score a few years ago. Oyvey!

The only real drawback to these cabinets is their size—four and a half to five feet wide—which, alas, is just too big for many rooms these days, but if you like to own things which are sure to rise in value (and who doesn't), these are a first-class buy for, although they have jumped recently, are still under-priced and have plenty of room for movement.

The lining of back and shelves will often be found to be a wee bit tatty but this should prove no great problem, for the shelves are normally easy to remove enabling the job to be accomplished quite simply.

EDWARDIAN DISPLAY CABINET

ALTHOUGH I have touched on specimen tables on an earlier page this particularly useful style from the Edwardian era has an additional upright display unit affixed to the top of the museum type display case.

It is made of mahogany with fine boxwood string inlay and crossbanding, has nicely glazed doors enclosing two adjustable shelves and is supported on square, tapering legs with spade feet. The horizontal display unit has a hinged top for easy access and is ideal for dis-

playing a collection of small articles like snuff boxes or vinaigrettes.

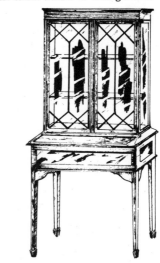

Edwardian display cabinet £175

111

A good reason for the high price of articles of this type is not so much their age as their value to dealers who find them ideal for displaying smaller bits and pieces in the shops since they take up little room, and most importantly, have locks on all doors.

If supermarket owners think they suffer as a result of the attentions of shoplifters, they should spend a week or two looking after an antique shop— all the world's magpies are attracted by the glitter of silver and crystal and it is small wonder that dealers prize these display cabinets so highly for, not only do they keep attractive items safely out of reach of sticky fingers, they also stand safely against the wall where those dreadful whirlwind people who spend their days knocking things over and breaking them (but never expect to pay for the damage they cause) cannot get at them too easily.

REGENCY CHIFFONIER

LATE in the 18th century, emphasis began to be placed on the lower parts of cabinets which, in the form of a rectangular structure with the addition of a shelf or two, became known as a chiffonier (a masculine version of the French chiffoniere—a small chest with legs).

These were made as a contrast to the larger sideboards and were used primarily for the storage of books or china and this particularly fine example, veneered in rosewood, has a delicate brass scroll inlay on the centre drawer and on the pilasters which rise each side of the brass-grilled door.

EDWARDIAN ROOM

In the early years of the twentieth century there was a movement of revolt against the Victorian tradition. This took the form of an art and craft movement led by William Morris, Charles Renee Mackintosh and designers such as C. F. A. Voysey, whose products can be seen in the room opposite.

Individually, many of the pieces from this period lack appeal but, seen as a complete room setting, they combine to create an air of artistic unity.

(Courtesy Geffrye Museum)

Regency chiffonier £300

These chiffoniers were made with a variety of feet; paw, scroll or, as illustrated, turned. This particular example has also a brass gallery mounted shelf but all of them command fair money since they are all beautifully made and extremely elegant pieces of furniture whether veneered in mahogany, rosewood or, at very best, satinwood.

19th CENTURY BOULLE CABINET

ALTHOUGH ebonised furniture is generally unpopular, a piece of the quality of this little cabinet is worthy of a place in any good home.

19th century Boulle cabinet £185

Just under three feet wide, this one has a glazed door enclosing a shelf and is finished with ormolu edging and mounts. But it is the Boulle decoration which is the real eye-catcher here. As mentioned earlier, Boulle decoration dates from the 17th century (Andre Charles Boulle lived from 1642 to 1732) and is usually found with either a black or a red ground—red being more expensive.

Boulle work is found on anything from tables to pianos and often has particularly attractive central panels decorated with delightful sylvan scenes. If the boulle is perfect, all is well but the trouble is that the intricate brass scrollwork has a habit of pinging up and this, to put it as mildly as I know how, is damned difficult to repair.

If it is simply a matter of reglueing pieces into place, life is not so bad but the real problems arise when fragments are missing.

The only solution I know of (and this is réally privileged information) is to buy a stick of beeswax the colour of the brass and a stick of sealing wax to match the tortoiseshell. The brass-coloured wax can be simply rubbed into the groove and polished up but the sealing wax needs careful application and a few streaks or blobs of black to achieve a convincing effect.

If this sounds a rather crude method of repair, all right—but I know of several pieces whose owners were never likely (till now) to suspect that some of their tortoiseshell came from Woolworths or W. H. Smith and Sons!

VICTORIAN BURR WALNUT CABINET

HERE is another dwarf cabinet of the same size and period as the previous piece but completely different in its decorative style. It owes much for its appearance to the Louis XVI designs but has an unmistakably early Victorian feeling about it.

Veneered in burr walnut, it has ormolu decoration including a mount in the centre of the door which surrounds a pictorial porcelain plaque. Other cabinets of the same period will be found sporting panels of floral marquetry executed in wood, ivory or bone and all were particularly popular throughout the 19th century when it was fashionable to hang a portrait above them or furnish the tops with clock sets or pairs of vases.

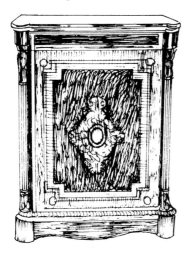

Victorian burr walnut cabinet £175

This cabinet shouldn't be confused with those that came from the later Victorian period, and were ebonised or veneered in plain walnut having a glazed door. These were nasty, grossly inferior boxes and worth only half the value of their predecessors.

If you don't trust your eye to judge the quality of these cabinets, try lifting them; the later models are light and flimsy whereas the real thing requires considerable effort and might give the impression that it is loaded with books or coal.

VICTORIAN MAHOGANY CHIFFONIER

Victorian mahogany chiffonier £75

114

ONE stage further and we have this mahogany chiffonier which, although Victorian, still possesses attributes of both the William IV and Regency periods preceeding it.

Loudon's *Encyclopaedia of Furniture* extolled the virtues of the chiffonier, describing it as "A most useful object for families who cannot afford to go to the expense of a pier or a consul table" which, judging from the numbers of chiffoniers still to be found, must have applied to something over 99 per cent of the population.

The shelved backboard has S scroll supports and the body of the piece is prettied up with applied, machine made mouldings in the rococo style. It has two drawers with cupboard doors below enclosing a shelf.

This is indeed a well-made piece of furniture, at its best veneered in rosewood, and is eminently more suited to modern rooms than many of the larger sideboards made in the same style.

VICTORIAN MAHOGANY CHIFFONIER

ALTHOUGH the shape of this piece is basically the same as that of the previous example, it is a different proposition altogether. Finished in uninspired mahogany or plain walnut veneers, it was cheaply made and badly constructed.

There is a single shelf on the backboard, which has applied rococo carving on the top, a shaped drawer and panelled doors; the whole supported on a plinth base. My only reason for recommending it is the price—inexpensive at the moment but unlikely to stay that way for too long.

There was, at Bermondsey Market, a particularly finnicky dealer who insisted on carrying out an almost microscopic examination of every piece catching his eye. This caused him to become rather unpopular with most other dealers who are, generally, very much of the "If you don't want me whelks don't muck 'em about" brigade, and who found his habits particularly irritating when they were busy with other customers.

One morning, he really upset the

dealer who had a stall two removed from mine by giving one of these chiffoniers a particularly tough going-over climaxing his act by actually climbing inside to inspect the interior. Without so much as a flicker, the stallholder closed the door and turned the key on him.

The poor little fellow had not been released when, some 15 minutes later, I was called away for a short time. When I returned the chiffonier had gone and the stallholder swore that he had sold it with the little fellow still inside.

If you should buy one of these and open it to find a short, curly headed man with glasses inside, please send him back to Bermondsey Market, London—his wife misses him.

Victorian mahogany chiffonier £25

DRAWING ROOM CABINET, CIRCA 1883

IF I may be allowed to express my opinion on the subject, the London Exhibition of 1861 has much to answer for because it was there that the swinging young designers of the 1860s were encouraged to show their "Art" furniture; a mistake which led to almost 50 years of hideous designs with only a few bright patches provided by people such as Morris.

The trouble was that the manufacturers, seeing the Art pieces, somehow decided that they could cash in by making cheap furniture and hiring artists to design Art bits which could be stuck on as fancy directed. What they achieved by this was a collection of ungainly, squarish constructions garnished with galleries, bedecked with bevelled mirrors and plastered with panels.

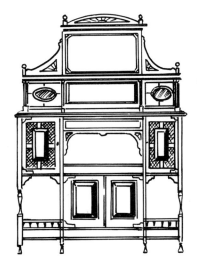

Drawing room cabinet, circa 1883 £20

As a general rule, these sorry monstrosities are ebonised or of plain walnut and, unfortunately, they were so strongly constructed that I am inclined to believe that every single one of them has survived to the present day—the only thing to have dropped off is the price; most are a few bob cheaper now than they were when they were new.

There were, however, a few manufacturers who, while making 18th century styled reproductions, made quantities of cabinets of this type in rosewood or mahogany inlaid with bone and ivory. While I am personally not enamoured of them, these are quite well worth their money which, at the moment, is about three times as much as the one I have quoted.

19th CENTURY ITALIAN CREDENZA

19th CENTURY WALNUT AND KINGWOOD CREDENZA

ALTHOUGH I have heard these items classed as anything from sideboards to chiffoniers, most dealers refer to them as credenzas. The word is Italian and applies to a long, low cabinet with up to four doors, a style which first made its appearance in this form during the last quarter of the 18th century.

They are quite large but have the virtue of combining the functions of various pieces of furniture, being suitable for displaying both china and silver while providing a covered storage area for less worthy pieces all under the same flat roof, as it were, which in turn is a very serviceable distance above the ground.

19th century Italian credenza (above) £500
19th century walnut and kingwood credenza (below) £500

The upper drawing is of an 19th century, gilded Italian credenza with gesso ornamentation and a shaped, figured marble top. It has glazed ends and fine pilasters on either side of the central door.

One thing that gilded cabinets of this style cannot stand is damp. This will cause the gilding to flake off and leave patches of red ochre ground showing underneath; in reasonable quantities, this effect can prove pleasantly harmonious and, in my view, not worth restoring but care should be taken to see that not too much gilding is lost, for this, as explained earlier, can be costly and difficult to replace.

The lower illustration is of a superb quality credenza, finished in burr walnut and kingwood with fine ormolu mounts and marquetry decoration on the doors.

VICTORIAN BREAKFRONT CREDENZA
19th CENTURY BURR WALNUT CREDENZA

THE upper illustration is of a breakfront credenza; that is, the cupboard protrudes forward of the line joining the glazed ends in a style which proved popular in bookcases made during the last quarter of the 18th century. Others have the central cupboard set back from the end pieces and these are known as inverted breakfronts, a style first seen in about 1790.

This particular credenza is veneered in burr walnut with ormolu mounts on the pilasters and a small amount of inlay in the centre door. As such, it is not over expensive, but similar pieces having inlaid flowers on the frieze and door can command two or three times the price.

The other piece has bowed ends and a panelled centre door which has a floral medallion with ormolu mounts and banding.

Don't be put off a piece because the bowed or serpentine glass in the ends is broken; replacing it with glass will prove very expensive but a piece of thin perspex will be found to bend to shape quite easily and will achieve the desired effect. Although perspex tends to scratch fairly easily and yellow slightly with age, any proprietary brand of metal polish will bring it up as good as new.

Victorian breakfront credenza (above) £275
19th century burr walnut credenza (below) £200

VICTORIAN EBONISED CREDENZA
LATE VICTORIAN EBONISED CREDENZA

EBONISED furniture became popular with new Art products being produced around the 1870s and, in a gallant attempt to give a new lease of life to some earlier styles, these too suddenly appeared on the market in an ebonised edition. This may have made money for the manufacturers but it did no favours to future generations (namely, us).

While the upper credenza here retains the same shape as that of the previous example, it was made about 30 years later and is of greatly inferior quality. Finished with gilt decoration on the door, the poor old thing has a token amount of brass embellishment to give it some appeal.

**Victorian ebonised credenza
(above) £85
Late Victorian ebonised credenza
(below) £75**

The last credenza is really the end. Have you ever seen anything looking more like a reject shop fitting? Someone, somewhere, must like these, however, for they always raise a few pounds at auction. Note the abundance of plate glass and the mirrored back to give the impression that it holds two of everything.

I find it quite nerve racking to move one of these, fully expecting it to sag into several sorry pieces at a touch. No such luck so far—perhaps a kick would do it.

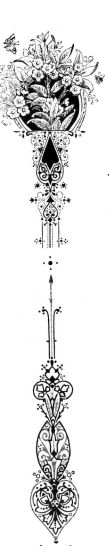

Sideboards

MOST pieces of furniture have clearly traceable roots planted firmly in the distant past. Not so the sideboard. In the form we know it today this particular item first appeared on the scene in or around 1770.

Prior to that time, certainly, there were sideboards (Chaucer—and who could argue with his evidence?—mentions a 'sytte borde') but these were no more than side tables, sometimes marble topped, which contained neither drawers nor cupboards.

The introduction of a sideboard as a piece of furniture designed for storage came about for one main reason; the hard drinking habits of 18th century Englishmen established a need for a convenient hidey hole in which to keep large quantities of booze close by the dining table. Dear old Robert Adam is on record as having said "The English, accustomed by habit, or induced by the nature of the climate, indulge more largely in the enjoyment of the bottle than the French." Which is as good a way as any of telling the world that his compatriots could drink a Frenchman sous la table any time they cared.

Personally, I have never been particularly enamoured of sideboards. They seem to me never to rise above being purely functional and largely unattractive lumps of furniture.

Designs vary enormously from the sublime to the "gor blimey", some being as long as the street while others are neat and compact. For this reason, anyone wanting a sideboard should not find it too difficult to find an antique piece which satisfies both eye and pocket.

PEDESTAL SIDEBOARD CIRCA 1785

IT is thought that Robert Adam was the first to couple the drawerless side table with a pair of pedestals, one to either end, often placing knife boxes on the top.

Although Shearer, on the other hand, usually takes the credit for joining the three sections together, as illustrated in his Guide of 1788, there are records of Messrs.Gillows informing one of their customers in 1779 that ". . . we make a new sort of sideboard table now, with drawers, etc., in a genteel style, to hold bottles. . . "

Chippendale, Sheraton and Hepplewhite, too, are all contenders for the title "Father of the Modern Sideboard" so, rather than become involved in pointless discussion, suffice it to say that the tail end of the 18th century was when it all happened and here is one of the earliest mahogany forerunners of your Danish teak job.

One of the pedestals houses a wine drawer and the other, a tin lined cupboard with racks for stacking plates.

There are some to be found which contain a pot cupboard in one of the pedestals. The door is usually quite inconspicuous and opens by means of a catch at the back. The only explanation I have ever heard for this quaint variation is that gentlemen, left by the ladies to put the world to rights over port and cigars, would sometimes prefer not to permit calls of nature to interrupt the conversation.

A nicer feature is the brass rail along the back which, apart from supporting dishes, often held a candelabra to throw light on to the plate.

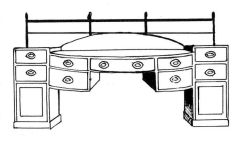

Pedestal sideboard, circa 1785 £300

BOWFRONTED SIDEBOARD
CIRCA 1785

THIS is one of the smaller bow-fronted sideboards intended for use in unpretentious, middle-income households.

While this one has four legs in the front, square and tapered with spade feet, and two at the back, slightly earlier sideboards of the type have only four legs altogether (one, would you believe, at each corner—like a cow).

The central drawer has curved under-framing and was intended for storing cutlery and table linen. It is flanked by either cupboards or deep drawers which were put to a number of uses, sometimes being partitioned for bottles, racked for plates or even lead lined to hold water in case a spot of quick washing up was required during the meal.

**Bowfronted sideboard
circa 1785   £400**

A good sideboard, this, made of fine mahogany and only about five feet wide—small enough to fit into most rooms quite easily.

Their small size and good quality accounts for the ample price fetched by the genuine pieces, but this style was reproduced at the end of the 19th century—indeed, it is still being reproduced today—and these pieces, although not as good from the point of view of the investor, represent quite good value for money, being considerably cheaper and often well made.

INLAID SIDEBOARD
CIRCA 1790

HERE is a mahogany sideboard of superb quality which has a straight front, bowed ends and is only five feet, two and a half inches long.

The square, tapering legs carry up-

ward to the top of the sideboard—a detail characteristic of the last decade of the 18th century—terminating in spade feet. The top is crossbanded with satinwood and the drawers have round, pressed handles but the feature which lifts this piece out of the commonplace is the elegant sufficiency of fine box-wood inlay work.

These, like many of the other late 18th century sideboards, were extensively reproduced during the closing years of the 19th century.

The inlaid central conch shell reminds me of one of the most spectacular buys at auction I have ever heard of.

It was the practice at the end of the 18th century for specialist marquetry manufacturers to supply cabinet makers with these motifs, along with fan, flower and urn shapes, ready for setting into suitable pieces of furniture.

Inlaid sideboard, circa 1790   £600

About 40 years ago, a dealer acquaintance of mine tells me, he purchased a mahogany trunk for a fiver at a country auction. Inside were some five thousand of these little pieces of inlay—the residual fruits of some long gone marquetry man's labours.

Not spectacular?

Try considering that the addition of an inlaid motif on a piece of furniture invariably adds at least a tenner to the price. . .

Spectacular.

CONCAVE FRONTED
SIDEBOARD, CIRCA 1790

ALTHOUGH Sheraton described the concave front as "not usual" for a sideboard, he was a great salesman

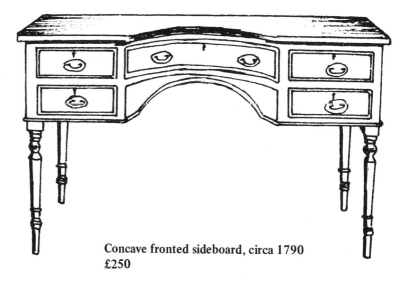

**Concave fronted sideboard, circa 1790
£250**

118

in his way and always ready to supply a practical justification for his design quirks.

Why give a sideboard a concave front ? Obvious.

A sideboards function is to stand near the kitchen door or serving hatch to save the servants bustling about all over the place during the meal. So what happens when the butler is standing at the sideboard preparing to buttle and all the waiters keep darting past, backward and forward ?

He nips into the concavity out of the way, doesn't he ?

It's a wonder that any other kinds of sideboards were ever sold !

Sheraton also observed that, being concave, the sideboard was easier to stretch across.

Apart from the inventiveness of the salestalk, this is a nicely proportioned piece, made of mahogany with fine turned legs and pressed brass handles.

BOWED END SIDEBOARD CIRCA 1795

THIS is a later version of the example before last, slightly larger (five feet, seven and a half inches wide) but not too large to fit into the average room.

Bowed end sideboard, circa 1795 £275

It is made of mahogany with six turned legs and oval, pressed brass handles and most probably had a brass rail at the back but, unfortunately, these will generally be found to have been removed—possibly because they are difficult to clean.

Sheraton illustrated a similar sideboard to this one in his Drawing Book of 1791, but his had a rectangular tablet in the centre of the middle drawer;

a device he often used to add a touch of distinction to his designs.

Following the normal practice for the last decade of the 18th century, the rounded ends of this sideboard each contain a single deep drawer whose fronts are panelled to give the apppearance of two drawers.

Another nice feature, also one of Sheraton's favourites, is the tambour fronted cupboard situated beneath the curved framing under the central drawer.

It is an odd fact that both my doctor and my dentist have one of these in their waiting rooms—a superstitious soul might think that there is something about this particular design which contains a secret healing power but it is far more likely to be an effect, rather than a cause, of their hippocratic success.

SHERATON HALF ROUND SIDEBOARD, CIRCA 1795

Sheraton half round sideboard circa 1795 £500

HERE is another Sheraton design which exemplifies his near obsession with concave and convex shapes.

A large piece which requires a large room around it, this is superbly made of mahogany and stands on only four square tapered legs.

The thing about these that particularly appeals to me is the way that the left hand drawer is sometimes fitted up as a plate warmer. There is a central rack on which the plates are placed and the inside of the drawer is lined with tin, as is the underside of the top. Beneath this drawer, whose bottom is left partially open, is another, narrow, drawer containing a heater with which to heat the plates. Of course, it may not get past your local Fire Prevention Officer these days but, knowing Sheraton (in a manner of speaking) it must

have worked reasonably efficiently.

In the price you get the brass rail at the back which might have a fitment for a pair of candelabra and would once have had little green silk curtains suspended from it. Sheraton had a thing about green silk curtains and, although he didn't originate the idea of their use, he certainly grasped every possible opportunity to employ them.

DOUBLE SERPENTINE FRONTED SIDEBOARD, CIRCA 1795

Double fronted serpentine sideboard circa 1795 £350

THIS is yet another shape for the front of a sideboard; not just your ordinary serpentine (a convex swell flanked by two concave curves) but a double serpentine—two convexes and three concaves—which adds up to a lot of sideboard; about nine feet of it, intended, according to the catalogue, for "a Nobleman's household".

It is made of mahogany with fine string inlay of either boxwood or holly and comes fitted with all 18th century mod. cons. including a cellarette, plate warmer, pot cupboard, tambour fronted cupboards and all, and all.

The legs are square tapered with spade feet, and not surprisingly, the mammoth bulk of the piece needs eight of them—four on each of the pedestal ends.

As usual with furniture, the smaller the sideboard, the better. The sheer unbelievable vastness of these pieces precludes their fetching anything like the price of their smaller, more stylish cousins, so, if you happen to be a nobleman in search of a sideboard for the ancestral hall, this is the kind of thing to go for if you want footage for your money.

It was Hepplewhite who, of all designers, particularly favoured the serpentine front, and it is a credit to him that a sideboard of this size manages to maintain an air of elegance—something that was lost when pedestal ends returned to ground level in the following century.

REGENCY SABRE LEG
SIDEBOARD, CIRCA 1805

SENSING a change of taste in the royal palaces, Thomas Sheraton, being a bright lad, was quick to publish some new designs in his *Cabinet Dictionary* of 1803. These were the first of what was to become known as the Regency style.

Riding on the crest of the wave, he followed his ideas up and, in his last publication (1804) we find chairs with shaggy lions' legs and camels forming the backs. So fantastic were these designs that some critics were prompted to hint that the fellow was losing his marbles. Perhaps they were right, for Sheraton died the following year, at the age of 55, of phrenitis—an inflammation of the brain.

Regency sabre leg sideboard, circa 1805   £400

Having said all that, I don't know who designed the sideboard illustrated above but, whoever it was, he made it in the style of the late 18th century and then, as a gesture to Sheraton, stuck sabre legs under the front.

Sabre legs look fine on chairs but have you ever seen a sideboard that looks more like a pantomime horse feigning drunkenness?

Mind you, put it in a dimly lit room with a set of sabre legged dining chairs and a twin pedestal table and you will find yourself the proud possessor of an extremely elegant eating place.

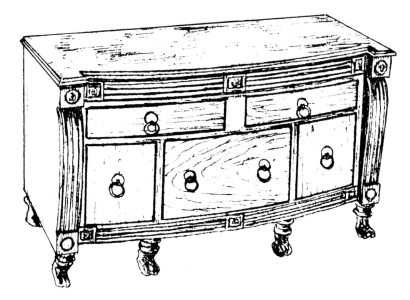

**Regency mahogany sideboard
circa 1815 £325**

REGENCY MAHOGANY
SIDEBOARD, CIRCA 1815

HOT on the heels of Sheraton came another Thomas, Hope, this time who, in his publication *Household Furniture and Interior Decoration*, established the English Empire style. This tended toward great bulk and solidity with maximum utilisation of space, but surprisingly, elegance was not altogether sacrificed.

Being anglicised versions of the French Empire style, these designs gained popularity when, after the defeat of Napoleon in 1812, English tourists could once again spend the few odd days in Paris. Cabinet makers of course, loved them, for their large flat surfaces free from carving and other decoration made them ideal for factory production lines.

Although the design of this mahogany sideboard, with its plain drawers, paw feet and metal mounted corbels leans heavily on Hope's ideas, the reeded front is straight from Sheraton.

PEDESTAL SIDEBOARD
CIRCA 1820

WITH the return, in the Regency period, of classical lines, sideboards underwent a change of style.

As a rule this meant a return of the old side table and pedestal arrangement but now these were made as a combined unit, with the cellarette drawers or cupboards extending downwards and the central drawer slightly protruding.

The sideboard illustrated is typical of the period, being made of mahogany or rosewood with tapering pedestal cupboards standing on paw feet.

The central shaped back piece was a characteristic innovation which, during the Victorian period to follow, was to develope into an extremely elaborate, and often beautiful feature.

The carcase is beautifully made and finished with brass or ebony inlay but, because of its somewhat foreboding Hammer film appearance, sadly lacks popular appeal at the moment.

Just occasionally a sideboard of this style will be found complete with a pair of knife boxes which were supplied with it to sit, one above each pedestal. This, however is quite rare nowadays owing to the fact that the knife boxes have for long been desirable items alone and are likely to fetch more than the sideboards to which they originally belonged.

Pedestal sideboard, circa 1820 £85

EARLY VICTORIAN SIDEBOARD

THIS slightly later sideboard, of mahogany or rosewood, is a logical development of the previous example and, like it, underpriced in my opinion.

It is superbly made, but because it is about six feet long and does not fit in with modern requirements, it has to suffer the indignities of a fallen aristocrat.

Early Victorian sideboard £55

It saddens me to look at furniture which has once held pride of place in the home being humped around auction rooms and knocked down for only a few pounds.

Someone should start a Society for the Prevention of Cruelty to Antiques. The purpose of the society would be to find Stately Homes for redundant goodies such as this, places where they would be carefully beeswaxed by menials on slave wages who would help themselves to the odd tot from the full cellarette and dust round the silver gracing their tops . . .

Funny how drink always makes some people sentimental.

VICTORIAN CARVED OAK SIDEBOARD, CIRCA 1840

Victorian carved oak sideboard circa 1840 £85

IT may have been partly as a result of the popularity of Sir Walter Scott's romantic historical novels that people felt the urge to break free from the classical restraint of the Regency period, turning for relief to the opulent extravagance of the Elizabethan styles of furniture, with their abundance of deeply carved decoration.

Whole rooms began to lose their formal elegance and, instead of keeping plenty of clear floor space with a few well chosen articles placed against the walls, furniture began creeping all over the place to such an extent that an exalted American wrote that English homes "were taking on the appearance of the upholsterers or Cabinet Makers' shops"

This piece is a nicely carved Victor-ian oak sideboard with lion's mask handles and paw feet.

And a very good buy, too, at the moment but going up as each month passes.

Most of the carving was in a naturalistic style depicting such mythological characters as Ceres and Bacchus, with attendant nymphs loaded with fruit, (particularly grapes), dead game birds and animals.

There are those lofty souls who may be heard to remark that the carving from this period is pretty poor stuff. Considering that this is, after all, decorative carving and not sculpture, I can only recommend that such people do as I have done—have a go at it themselves—they might then become aware of what bad carving really is, conclude that scoffing is pretty easy and begin to appreciate what they see,

VICTORIAN BURR WALNUT SIDEBOARD, CIRCA 1850

THIS little sideboard dates from the middle of the 19th century—that brief oasis of good taste in a wilderness of monumental error—and was made along with the superb quality cabriole leg chairs , davenports and loo tables which typify the decade, of burr walnut in the rococo style.

Slightly fussy for some tastes, perhaps, but this sideboard exudes an air of pleasant frivolity which was soon to be stamped out under the weight of the bigger, more masculine furniture styles lurking just a few years away.

Victorian burr walnut sideboard circa 1850 £90

The shaped open shelves flank a central cupboard which also houses a shelf and the decorative flower carving is naturalistic in style. There is a small mirror in the shaped backboard, and good examples are sometimes found to be inlaid with boxwood.

The size of this pleasant little sideboard (four feet six inches wide) ensures its continuing popularity and is well worth buying as an investment.

VICTORIAN SIDEBOARD CIRCA 1860

THIS style of sideboard has been hovering on the popularity fringe for about a year now, and is, I feel sure, just about to zoom up in price. As soon as that happens, of course, they will be difficult to find.

Victorian sideboard circa 1860 £55

Their main disadvantage lies in their size—about six feet wide, seven feet high, but they are so distinctively styled that I cannot believe that they will not be made to fit somewhere into the rooms of today.

This one was made about 1860, of burr walnut, in the French rococo style of flowing lines and applied carving, the whole topped by a D shaped mirror in a carved frame. Later pieces were finished in plain walnut or a rather dull uninteresting mahogany and are not nearly so pleasant to look at.

To complete the image of distinction, sideboards of this type usually sport

fine, white marble tops. These are cut to follow the contours of the fronts, which are many and varied but always based on a series of contrasting curves and the mirror is relied upon to tie the whole design together and give it some sort of unity.

MID VICTORAIN PEDESTAL SIDEBOARD, CIRCA 1870

Mid Victorian pedestal sideboard circa 1870 £40

NEVER mind the sideboard, just look at that backboard !

A few years prior to this time, large mirrors had been hung above the sideboards of the nation but now, with the backboards becoming an increasingly important feature of the piece, designers seem to have considered the sideboard as little more than a useful support for half an acre of plate glass mirror whose function was probably to double the apparent number of voguish sideboard dishes placed before it.

At first, the integral mirrors were arranged in threes— a larger rectangle in the centre flanked by smaller ones above the pedestals. This quickly developed through the rococo delights into the form illustrated left.

This sideboard is made of mahogany and has applied rococo carving on the pedestal doors which seems to have been some kind of concession to the mirror frame above—a small acknowledgement that the two pieces are, indeed, related.

It will be seen that the central area between the pedestals has been enclosed by means of panelled doors behind which there is a shelf. The wine cooler which had previously occupied this space had fallen from popularity and was being made as a separate piece of furniture for those who felt in need of it.

A superb nineteenth century burr walnut credenza with marquetry inlay and heavy ormolu mounts.   £800

122

LATE 19th CENTURY SIDEBOARD

THIS rather strange looking display sideboard became popular towards the end of the 19th century and remained in favour throughout the Edwardian era.

Late 19th century sideboard
ebonised £20
mahogany £35
inlaid £85

There is clear evidence of the rococo influence in the cabriole legs, shaped apron and flowing back but the piece is unmistakably a brainchild of an enthusiastic, turn of the century designer. A number of variations on this theme were made over the years and these came in a variety of finishes from good quality mahogany to repulsively ebonised firewood. I prefer the fine, red mahogany pieces which are still to be found and which, I think, have a certain charm lacking in most others.

Although I say I prefer the red mahogany version, none of them are really to my taste and the best are really those which are inlaid delicately with bone and ivory in representations of grotesque masks amid foliate scrolls. Sometimes the entire thing is further embellished with quantities of brass beading.

As far as recommendation goes, the ebonised version burns well, the plain mahogany type is quite interesting and the inlaid model is definitely worth the money and merits a place alongside the best of furniture from its period—just so long as it is not in my home.

LATE 19th CENTURY SIDEBOARD

ALTHOUGH most of the late Victorian sideboards are rather lacking in aesthetic appeal, commercial cabinet makers such as Gillows were tireless in their quest for novel ideas with which to capture the imaginations of their clients.

The two most successful styles were those of the late 18th century and of the Italian Renaissance.

The latter was a grand, architectural style, elegant in detail and elaborately designed to include brackets, shelves, niches and cupboards. Critics referred to these pieces as being in the "Bracket and overmantel style".

They were smothered in a surfeit of mirrors, inlaid panels, plaques and any other bits and pieces of frippery which the cabinet maker had to hand. Their carcases are large and exotic—the piece illustrated is six feet wide by eight feet, two and a half inches tall and is made of ebony and amboyna.

Late 19th century sideboard £500

Although this is a fine example of its type, its size makes it a non starter in most homes, which is a shame because the quality is superb.

What a pity it is that, with all the craftmanship and expertise employed in the manufacture of these fairytale pieces, there were not some made to more reasonable proportions.

LATE 19th CENTURY INLAID SIDEBOARD

A WEE bit fussy, this one, with its jumble of levels, but it is extraordinarily well made even though its decorative value outweighs its usefulness.

Late 19th century inlaid sideboard £90

Veneered in rosewood, the piece has marquetry decoration of bone and ivory in the form of foliate scrolls. The cupboard brackets are arched and the spindle supports lift the body of the sideboard to a respectable height above the pot board. Once again, these were made to a size that precludes their adoption in most modern households for, despite their delicate appearance, sideboards of this type are invariably about six feet wide by seven high.

These pieces come in a variety of shapes and sizes (all large) and all have mirrors and baluster turned galleries incorporated into their design somewhere.

Although I cannot agree with the practice, I have seen these dismembered to make a low sideboard of the base section with the mirror adapted for hanging and the little cupboards converted into wall fittings. A great pity but there seems to be no reasonable alternative.

LATE 19th CENTURY SIDEBOARD

THIS sorry creature lacks both decorative appeal and usefulness which means, in short, that it has very little going for it.

Although it is based on a similar design to that of the previous example, something, somewhere went wrong and we are left with a dull, cumbersome lump made of a variety of woods from solid mahogany to oak and American walnut. There is a bevelled glass back, a row of three drawers in the frieze and a pair of carved and panelled cupboard doors, one of which encloses a cellarette. It has a token amount of low relief carving, is about seven feet wide and would have cost precisely £33 when new in 1885—without Green Shield stamps.

Late 19th century sideboard £15

If I still haven't put you off and you feel that this is for you; congratulations! you will certainly get your money's worth. But don't buy it as an investment unless you are prepared to gamble on the chance that your great great grandchildren might make a few bob on it.

The usual fate of most sideboards of this type is to be cast on to Corporation rubbish dumps and, if you are unlucky enough to inherit one and feel that this is the only solution, may I suggest that you first remove all handles, fittings and carved panels, pop them into a box and stick them in the attic, cellar, garage or toolshed (or wherever else you hoard junk).

I have not the faintest idea of what could be done with them but it would be a waste to just chuck them out willy nilly.

EDWARDIAN SIDEBOARD

HERE'S another of the pieces I love to hate. The only good thing I can say about it and its kind is that they are exported in large quantities.

Edwardian sideboard £25

The Americans, though, must want them, for that's where they all go but I can't believe that even Americans like them as they are—perhaps they bleach them or paint stars and stripes across them

Apart from the appalling design, this sideboard is not too bad—in fact it is very well constructed of a rich red mahogany with a bevelled glass back—but it is so heavy and dull. Strangely, there are a few hints of art nouveau features here and there but these are weighted down and restricted in a manner that is quite criminal.

Amazingly, a piece of this type and quality would have cost between £40 and £50 at the turn of the century—and that was when money was money.

The only idea (which has just occurred to me) which might reasonably account for the numbers of these that are exported is that they make cheap packing cases for the quantities of fragile glass and china travelling regularly across the Atlantic.

JACOBEAN STYLE SIDEBOARD CIRCA 1920

THE end of a long and arduous war left a large section of the population of Britain hungry for security and feeling a need to get down to basics and start again. This is clearly reflected in the sudden upsurge of popularity of furniture made in good, old fashioned styles of good old fashioned oak.

During this period, a mahogany finish was described derisively as "stained and sticky looking" and the new art overmantels "pretentiously fussy and a haven for ineffable green grotesques of cats and other depressing forms of pottery". So there.

The Jacobean style was what people wanted and was soon adapted for mass production methods but, alas, experienced craftsmen were few and quality suffered accordingly.

This piece of furniture, although I think of it as a sideboard, was originally described in the catalogue as a dresser. It is made of dark oak and has a cane panelled back.

More likely to be found in a second hand furniture shop than an Antiques Gallery, the piece is very reasonably priced.

All right, I know it is not one of your top quality investment pieces and won't go with the colour telly too well, but put it in a cottagey atmosphere with a few matching pieces and you might be surprised at how good it looks.

Jacobean style sideboard, circa 1920 £25

 # INDEX

FINIS